Essentials of
Classroom Teaching
Elementary Science

Essentials of Classroom Teaching
Elementary Science

Robert J. Beichner
North Carolina State University, Raleigh

Daniel C. Dobey
State University College of New York, Fredonia

SERIES DEVELOPER
C. Alan Riedesel
State University of New York at Buffalo

Allyn and Bacon
Boston London Toronto Sydney Tokyo Singapore

Editor-in-Chief, Education: Nancy Forsyth
Series Editorial Assistant: Christine Nelson
Cover Administrator: Linda Dickinson
Composition Buyer: Linda Cox
Manufacturing Buyer: Louise Richardson
Editorial-Production Service: Colophon Production Service
Cover Designer: Suzanne Harbison
Text Designer: LeGwin Associates

Copyright © 1994 by Allyn and Bacon
A division of Paramount Publishing
160 Gould Street
Needham Heights, Massachusetts 02194

Library of Congress Cataloging-in-Publication Data
Beichner, Robert J.
     Essentials of classroom teaching: elementary science/Robert Beichner, Daniel C.
Dobey.
          p.   cm.
     Includes bibliographical references and index.
     ISBN 0-205-14579-5
     1. Science—Study and teaching.   2.Science—Study and teaching (Elementary)
I. Dobey, Daniel C.   II. Title.
Q 181.B435   1993   93-36942
372.3'5—dc20   CIP

Q
181
.B435
1994

Printed in the United States of America
10   9   8   7   6   5   4   3   2   99   98   97   96   95

Contents

Preface

"We will be number one in the world in math and science by the year 2000." So spoke then President George Bush in 1988. Since then, a significant movement has occurred to revitalize elementary school science teaching in the United States. Science education pedagogy, curriculum reform, and science teacher preparation have been a source of focus in colleges and schools across the country.

In *Essentials of Classroom Teaching: Elementary Science* we invite you to make hands-on, minds-on science teaching a reality. Each chapter highlights Science Teaching Activities to Try with various age groups of children. Each chapter also includes Science Teaching Vignettes so that you can observe the interactions between and among children and their science teachers as they DO science. As you read these prompts for hands-on, minds-on science teaching remember that, just as children must construct their own understanding of science, the pre-service science teacher must also construct his or her own understanding of science and science teaching pedagogy. By focusing on Science Teaching Activities to Try and Science Teaching Vignettes, we offer a realistic approach to teaching elementary school science.

Notable features of *Essentials of Classroom Teaching: Elementary Science* includes Looking Ahead which offers a preview and rationale of each chapter which lies ahead. At the beginning of each chapter Can You questions stimulate your thinking and discussing of salient science teaching topics before you read about them. Looking Back succinctly summarizes and reviews the main points of the chapter. Each science content chapter (chapters 5-9) includes a Scope and Sequence of the different topics of a particular science discipline and at what grade level they might be taught. The science content chapters also offer understandable explanations to many of those perplexing science questions that children ask (and teachers want to know)! Looking Ahead which offers a preview and rationale of each chapter which lies ahead. Finally, each chapter concludes with a Self-Test, References from Research and a list of Practical Resources that will provide you with further information.

Perhaps the most striking physical feature of *Essentials of Classroom Teaching: Elementary Science* is that it is much shorter than the usual comprehensive text for an elementary science methods course. This smaller size is an intentional design feature. Calls for reform have included recommendations that pre-service teachers spend more time in field experiences. As courses have been restructured to permit more field experience, there has often been a corresponding decrease in the amount of time spent in the college classroom. This has led to a tendency to under-utilize the comprehensive methods texts that were designed for college-classroom-based courses. We have had to make many difficult decisions in writing this text; there is so much one could say about teaching elementary school science. However, it is our intent that this text will meet the needs of today's field-based courses more precisely than would a more comprehsive text. We do not pretend that a 200-page text provides all of the material that is necessary. We urge the instructor to supplement *Essentials of Classroom Teaching: Elementary Science* with readings from the general methods text of this series and from some of the current research references and practical resource references that are listed at the end of each chapter in our text.

Before we close, many thanks to those college and school teacher colleagues who have shared their expertise with us and now you. To J. Adams, J. Brown, S. Jasalavich, L. Maheady, B. Mallette, W. Peruzzi, S. Raimondi, L. Schafer, J. Sexton and D. Wood - THANK YOU!

One final thought — GOOD SCIENCE TEACHING!

Essentials of Classroom Teaching
Elementary Science

1 Today's Elementary Science Classroom

LOOKING AHEAD

This chapter is not so much a description of the "typical classroom" as it is a discussion of a type of learning atmosphere or ambiance. As you might expect, there exists a tremendous variety of classroom environments, even within the same school building. You will certainly need to adjust to—and modify—the surroundings you find yourself in at the start of the school year. Of course, there are certain practical limits to what you can do, usually resulting from budgetary and political constraints. Nonetheless, there are some things that you can do to make the setting you and your students work in reflect your own philosophies of teaching and learning. This chapter is simultaneously a proposal for one such philosophy and an encouragement for you to find your own. There are many ways to teach science. You should keep as many of them as possible in your "teacher's toolbox."

CAN YOU?

Look over the "Can You?" questions at the beginning of each chapter to get a feel for what will follow. Read the chapter and then come back and add to your answers as necessary. Obviously, many of the ideas will be new to you, so don't expect to know everything right away. Nevertheless, thinking about the ideas before reading helps everything fit together later. Besides, bringing up interesting questions for investigation turns out to be a central tenet of our favorite way of teaching science!

SO, CAN YOU?

- Describe how the problems approach to teaching science capitalizes on the common characteristic of children to constantly ask, Why?

- State how the problems approach model of teaching differs from more traditional teaching techniques?

- Make up a couple of questions students might ask after coming in from an outside recess period?

- Indicate how questions might lead to science activities?

- Think how you might help students with their science activities?

- Define science based on what you were taught about it in elementary school?

- State how your current understanding of science is any different than what you learned as a youngster?

- Remember any science that you learned in elementary school?

- Give any reasons why you might not remember much science that was taught to you in elementary school?

OBSERVING THE PROBLEMS APPROACH IN ACTION

Let's begin by looking at an example of a classroom situation that reflects some of the teacher-student interactions that will be promoted in this text. Consider the following dialogue:

Sally: Ms. Sanchez, can you help me with a science problem?

Ms. Sanchez: Sure! Maybe the class can help, too. What is it?

Sally: Well, my aunt and uncle spent the night at our house last night. At breakfast this morning I noticed that my aunt puts cream in her coffee right away. My mom always lets hers cool a little first, then puts in the cream. I asked her and she says it ends up cooling faster that way.

Ms. Sanchez: So what's the problem?

Sally: Who's right? I mean, they are saying opposite things.

Ms. Sanchez: Can you put what they are saying into different words? Maybe that would make it easier to find a solution.

Sally: Well . . . my aunt says hers cools off faster than mom's.

Ms. Sanchez: OK. How can you tell when something is cooling off?

Sally: Its temperature goes down . . . so all we have to do is use a thermometer to see which is coolest.

Ms. Sanchez: Is there anything else we have to look at?

Sally: I don't think so . . . .

Leo: Ms. Sanchez, won't that just tell us the temperature? How do you tell which cools off the *fastest*?

Sally: We have to make a couple measurements to find out how fast the temperature drops!

Ms. Sanchez: Exactly what measurements have to be taken? Yes, Maria?

Maria: You have to measure the temperature in both cups before you start. That has to be the same to make it fair. Then let her aunt put in some cream. Wait a couple minutes and then have her mom put cream in her cup, just like she always would. Then all you have to do is measure both temperatures at the same time to find out who wins!

Sally: Can I borrow a couple thermometers, Ms. Sanchez? I'll be real careful with them!

Ms. Sanchez: I think that would be okay.

Leo: Can I, too?

Ms. Sanchez: Sure. Why don't you and Sally do the experiment at home with your parents, compare notes, then tell everybody what happened. Then we'll all see if we can come up with some other experiments we can do in class that might help us better understand what you find out.

You may have noticed that this interaction between the teacher and her students is a long way from a lecture on the Law of Cooling or a worksheet on Fahrenheit/Celsius temperature conversions!

Probably the key to the whole discussion comes right at the beginning. The teacher was open to adjust her own plans when she saw the opportunity for a student-motivated science lesson. Ms. Sanchez did not immediately supply the answer. (In fact, she may not have known which cup was going to "win!") Instead, she guided her students through an elaboration of the problem and the creation of a plan for finding the solution by careful observation, recording of data, and a collaboration of effort. These findings were to be shared with the other students. Last, but not least, more experiments were to be planned to further everyone's understanding of the problem.

From this brief discussion, what can we learn about the kind of classroom Ms. Sanchez runs? Well, it appears that her students are willing to bring in questions, share their ideas, and work together. There must be a respect for others that permeates all aspects of the class. Students take risks by raising questions, even if those questions might seem silly or trivial. The teacher takes risks by being open to those questions. How might Ms. Sanchez establish this kind of rapport? Sometimes she lets her students freely talk back and forth, other times she selects who will speak next. How do you suppose she decides whether to let a student speak without being called on? Can you detect how she deals with incomplete answers from her students?

You might wonder what kind of planning this impromptu science lesson requires. Actually, quite a lot is required. In order to really be comfortable with the flexibility demanded by her openness to student questions, Ms. Sanchez must be willing to learn more about science herself. There is no telling what questions students might ask a teacher who is willing to help them find answers! There is certainly no way to know the answers in advance. A good science background is important, but often the teacher must be able to locate information on a new topic. Having reference materials within easy reach is important. The school's library can provide good reference materials. There are several good one-volume *Encyclopedia of Science*-type books and a number of good science trade books that provide information on specific science topics. If the teacher has access to computers, there are several ways technology can help. For example, there is a single compact disc-sized CD-ROM that contains nearly 1,000 science lesson plans. This software enables the teacher to locate specific lessons by many criteria, including grade level, topic, and skills required. This might make it easier to come up with a quick but well-designed lesson related to something the students brought up. If the school has a modem, the teacher might be able to contact other teachers in the area (or even across the country) to see if any of them have helpful suggestions. Regardless of what resources are available, the preplanning required for a lesson like that described at the beginning of this chapter is a knowledge of what is available and how to use it rapidly.

Once the students have begun their activities, the teacher may want to conduct a few trials herself. Certainly this will acquaint her with any pitfalls her students might encounter. It also directly gives her the answer to the question from the ultimate authority—nature itself. Ms. Sanchez, in this case, and you in your own classroom must be prepared to give up the role of unquestioned authority figure. In science, people are not the final arbiters. Careful observations of nature provide the solutions.

Notice that some of the traditional parts of planning—mapping out all the activities of the students, for example—is not done by the teacher. Obviously, she must have input into what her students do, but a large part of the science lesson is the students' planning of what kind of experiment to run. This relieves a great deal of the burden of planning from the teacher's shoulders. However, it places a premium on flexibility and creativity. Once the students report their findings, the whole class, with the teacher, will need to be able to work together to develop more questions for study. These can be recorded during a class brainstorming session. Does adding cool water have the same effect as adding cream? How about adding cool coffee, instead? If the teacher wants to carry the lesson further, she can suggest that students examine how cup shape might change the cooling rate. This would be an excellent time to show students how a thermos works. Coming up with these kinds of additional questions requires substantial commitment on the teacher's part. Don't think that having students plan some of their own activities will free you from responsibility. Use your greater experience and access to resources to provide them with interesting things to discover and think about. Offer suggestions and probe their thinking with questions. The trick lies in balancing what you want to cover with the questions students bring in. That's not always easy!

WHAT IS SCIENCE? WHO IS A SCIENTIST?

On our way to developing a philosophy or schema for teaching science, we need to carefully examine two concepts. We must answer the questions "What is teaching?" and "What is science?" We will find that these two ideas interact strongly. Let's start with the latter because our definition of science will heavily influence how we might teach the subject. The first thing you might want to know is what you should be teaching. Unfortunately, even though our starting point is obvious—defining science—coming up with a definition is not nearly as easy as you might think.

You might remember your own school days when you were taught something called the "Scientific Method." At the time, it probably seemed quite formidable-hypothesis generation, experimentation, prediction. Certainly, it was nothing that you would ever be able to do on your own! The impression left by this view is that a scientist pulls a checklist out of a white lab coat pocket, marks off the task just completed, notes the next step, and goes back to work. In the real world of science, things aren't nearly so clear-cut and dry.

> **Scientists are problem posers and problem solvers.**

Scientists ask questions about the world and the things in it. They are curious, but they also *act* on their curiosity. They try to find the answers to their questions. Sometimes they systematically follow the Scientific Method—a way of finding out. Sometimes they work by a haphazard sort of trial and error. Much of the time, though, scientists are between these two extremes. They are guided by intuition and their own background knowledge of the area they are studying. Sometimes the path toward a solution is straightforward. Oftentimes it is not. Nonetheless, they search for ways to solve a problem presented by nature. Occasionally their models of the world stack tightly together like a set of Lego® bricks. Other times, the models collapse when an underlying assumption can't be verified. Every so often a theory gets so unwieldy that the only way to make progress is to tear it apart and start over again. If this process sounds like the way children play, it is! Young children seem to be blessed with the curiosity and tenacity of any of our best scientists. Watch a little one grappling with the law of gravity while learning to walk. Observe the wonder in a youngster's eyes as the child looks at a spider web glistening with dew. Children, by their very nature, are curious about their surroundings. That's also the prime characteristic of scientists. Unfortunately, the few people who manage to become professionals in a scientific career are able to do so only because they could ward off the stifling of their inborn curiosity. The fact that many adults dislike science is actually a condemnation of some of our methods of teaching science.

Anyway, back to the original question: What is science?

Science is the enterprise of learning about specific aspects of our surroundings.

Science includes careful observation driven by curiosity. An additional facet of science is the sharing of findings and ideas. In the world of the scientist, the results of a study are subjected to a review by other scientists. Only after the research passes this test is it published as part of the body of knowledge for that field. It is this important communications aspect that really makes one a scientist and not just a casual observer. This concept of working together and sharing ideas is what must be stressed in the classroom. Too often, students think (and have been told) that this is cheating. Certainly there are times when students need to work alone, but one of the prerequisite skills of adult life is being able to work cooperatively with others. If we feel that preparation for adulthood is an important part of education, then we have an obligation to impart the skills necessary for a successful, enjoyable adult life. That includes the ability to participate in group activities. Take a look at the following Science Activity to Try and see how first graders can find out about their natural world.

SCIENCE ACTIVITY TO TRY

AUTUMN SPLENDOR: LEAVES

The spectacular beauty of autumn just beckons your first graders outside to observe and find out about the annual rites of fall—leaves of deciduous trees turning their beautiful shades of red, orange, and yellow.

Title: Autumn Leaves

Skills: Observing, recording, classifying

Content: Colors, shapes, relative size, common plants and their leaves

Materials: Paper bags, magnifying glasses, chart paper

Procedure: Divide children into teams of two and give each team a paper bag. Go outside and collect leaves. When the children have finished collecting leaves, come inside and discuss the different ways of grouping the leaves (e.g., color, size, shape). Hand out chart paper to each team and have them record their color and size results.

Color a box for each leaf.

COLOR OF LEAVES							
RED							
YELLOW							
ORANGE							
BROWN							
GREEN							

Write the correct number for each size.

SIZE OF LEAVES	
BIG	
LITTLE	

Make a bulletin board classroom classification collage and place leaves on it according to shape.

Closure: Ask the children to show and describe their most beautiful leaf. Ask "What happens to leaves in autumn?"

As will be seen in chapter 4, there are several complementary aspects of science with which we need to be concerned. First, **science has provided us with a body of knowledge**—certain facts that have been ascertained from experimentation and observation. Second, **there are technical skills required in order to accumulate additional scientific knowledge**. These skills are sometimes called the *processes* of science. They include observation skills and the ability to use specialized measuring instruments. Finally, **there are certain attitudes that scientists cultivate**. Obviously, curiosity is the starting point. It also is important to be open-minded about new ideas. One must be able to hold back judgments until sufficient evidence has accumulated to justify acceptance or rejection of an idea. In addition, a healthy skepticism is also a desirable characteristic. Richard P. Feynman, a Nobel prize-winning physicist with a keen interest in elementary school science, once stated, "Science is the belief in the ignorance of experts." (What does he mean by this?) Scientists strive for objectivity, attempting to minimize their own biases. This sometimes requires them to abandon pet theories. It always means presenting findings to other scientists for their review.

PRINCIPLES OF TEACHING ELEMENTARY SCHOOL SCIENCE

What Is Teaching and How Does it Relate to Science?

Teachers provide a learning environment for their students. That's all they can do. They can't force facts into children's heads, although they can motivate the students to study. They can't build the synapses in a student's brain that relate two concepts, but they can show the student how the ideas go together. Here's the hard part: They shouldn't be the final authority on any specific scientific fact. This is where teachers have trouble. They recall the teacher-student relationship of their own school days. The all-knowing teacher stood at the front of the room and lectured to attentive children seated in neat, parallel rows of desks. Well, today's students, as new teachers quickly find out, have a different view of authority. Rather than set yourself up for a year-long battle for control, give your students the opportunity to think for themselves. Give them the means to evaluate the ideas and actions of others. Show them how to critically examine their surroundings. Then build up their confidence so that they are willing to share their thoughts with others. (At this point, you may want to refer back to our definition of science for an interesting coincidence.)

Children Can Be Problem Posers and Investigators
By now you can begin to see the connection between children's natural curiosity and scientific endeavors. What is important to establish in the classroom is an awareness of the fact that science surrounds us. Any time you wonder how something works or why things happen the way they do, you are really posing a scientific problem. By promoting this, your students will begin to realize that they have been acting like scientists all their lives and could realistically pursue science as an enjoyable, rewarding career. To get them started, you need to teach them to be observant in a systematic way. Use their natural interest in the world as a motivation for learning even more.

What Is the Problems Approach to Teaching Science?
One of the philosophies raised as a model in this text is the *problems approach to* teaching. In it, students are encouraged to raise questions about the world around them. These self-generated problems are used as a mechanism for guiding the development of scientific attitudes, the development of skills, and the learning of science facts.

Of course, not all the questions come from the students. It is the teacher's primary responsibility to generate interesting and thought-provoking ideas for the students to investigate. The fact that science is all around us, coupled with the natural curiosity of children, means that it is fairly easy to create science-oriented questions that the students have already puzzled over. Once a problem has been identified, it is up to the students to develop a plan to solve the problem or answer the question. The teacher at this point acts as an assistant—relieving some of the burden of traditional preparation, but adding other responsibilities. This model is a far cry from having students simply read from their textbooks and then fill in the blanks on worksheets. You have to decide if you are willing to give up directly imparting a little factual knowledge for an increase in enthusiasm and longer term recall of what is learned. In other words, do you want the children to be able to regurgitate lots of facts (only to forget them right after the test), or do you want them to get excited about all the interesting things around them and to be willing (and able) to find out more about their world? In the long term, which do you think is more valuable?

Actually the decision is even easier than that. It's not an all-or-nothing proposition. For example, you certainly cannot exclude instruction of science vocabulary words because your students are too busy "exploring." Luckily it doesn't have to be that way. By letting children investigate problems of interest to them (regardless of whether they bring them in to you or you present questions to them), you will see the side benefit that they end up learning what you wanted them to learn anyway. In fact, they will find it easier to memorize facts because those facts now have intrinsic, real-life meaning. It isn't just a rote memory task. The science concepts fit into a web of ideas, each one partly supporting and being supported by the others. You'll find out more about this connectedness of concepts in the next chapter.

The Teacher's Role Is as a Guide
Sometimes students will bring questions into the classroom. Other times, especially at the beginning of the year, you must put the children into situations that help them come up with questions. In all probability, they have never been in a classroom where they were given the opportunity to explore things that interested them. This may have already partly stunted their intellectual growth. You need to overcome this unnatural inertia starting to develop in their thought processes. Tease questions out of them by surrounding them with a stimulating environment. Raise seemingly paradoxical situations or startle them with an unexpected or discrepant event. (Having children roll steel ball bearings across a table that secretly has a magnet taped to the underside is one of our favorites!) You'll find that as the year progresses, they will be generating more and more questions—and thinking up ways to find the answers! Write

down some of their best ideas and you'll have a start on next year's science classes.

Nature Is the Authority

This is the hardest part of the whole problems approach to teaching philosophy. It's the hardest for the teacher, anyway; students don't have any problem with it! You must be able to give up your ego-satisfying, emotionally safe role as authority figure. Scientists in ancient Greece sat in the shade and made pronouncements about the world around them. We are a bit more sophisticated now. Since Galileo, experimentation has been a vital part of science. Nature has the answers to the questions we raise about it. We just have to come up with a way of getting nature to give up those secrets.

There Are No Right or Wrong Answers, Only Careful Observations

Because of the experiential basis of finding answers to questions, there are no simple right or wrong answers. Whatever nature "did" during an experiment is what should have—in fact, *must have*—happened. It may not answer the question originally posed because of poor measurement techniques or an incomplete gathering of data, but it is the way the world responds to the student's probing. The key here is teaching children to be careful and thorough in their investigations. This is how they start on the journey toward becoming mature adults in a scientifically oriented world.

Hands-On/Minds-On Experience Is a Must

Elementary school students have short attention spans, especially after years of bombardment from television. On top of this, we must keep in mind that most children at this age understand concrete ideas easier than they grasp abstract concepts. Luckily, they are "designed" to enjoy manipulating things to find out how they work and to learn more about them. Watch a baby explore a colorful rattle when it is first presented. Older children use this talent in their play, also. You might want to think about why children play in the first place.

It is your job to provide a stimulating environment for your children to explore. Science is things—lots of them. If it sounds like you must provide a playroom, well, maybe you should. The "toys" would not necessarily be the kind that children hope for on their birthdays (although there is plenty of good science in them!). Rather, you should set up interesting and exciting situations designed to pique your students' curiosity about scientific topics. If you can see the science found in everyday objects, so much the better. You can show your students how to notice the same things. However, if you don't know how a television makes white from red, green, and blue screen dots, don't give up hope! There are lots of places to find out about such delicious tidbits. Later, we'll talk about where you can go for help.

Attitude Building Is Important
Talk to a typical high school student about science and you might discover a shocking change from the curiosity the student had as a young child. In his or her mind, science has probably come to be thought of as a particular class and a specific teacher—unfortunately, maybe something or someone he or she didn't like! The idea that science exists outside the classroom and might be of interest to someone other than a "nerd" is foreign to a high school student. We want to avoid that attitude and we must work hard during the student's formative years to show him or her the wonders of science and scientific endeavors. We must foster the natural curiosity of students and help them develop it into a mature inquisitiveness that will make their adult lives more full. Being their teacher at the elementary level gives you the chance to make a big difference in their lives and in their approach to things and ideas new to them. You can make a difference!

LOOKING BACK

The problems approach to teaching science should be one of the main tools in your toolbox of techniques. Bringing up interesting questions or situations and being flexible in topical coverage capitalizes on the natural curiosity of children. By being willing to give up some of your authority, you can teach children to trust in themselves and to seek out answers on their own. As true scientists, they learn to discover solutions to their questions about the world around them from nature itself. Foster their independent thinking and critical observation. As someone once said, "Be the guide at their side, not the sage on the stage!" Work to nurture and strengthen their natural curiosity. Let them come up with their own questions and find out for themselves!

SELF-TEST

This might be a good time to go back and look at your answers to the focus questions at the beginning of the chapter.

- How have your ideas about science and teaching changed?

- How does the problems approach to teaching science fit into your teaching personality?

- What is the importance of hands-on activities to elementary school science teaching?

- What is your role as the teacher in a problems approach oriented science program?

- Why is building positive student attitudes so important in teaching?

PRACTICAL RESOURCES

Brooks, J. (1990). Teachers and students: constructivists forging new connections. *Educational Leadership*, 47(5), 73–78.

Driver, R. (1983). *The pupil as scientist*? Philadelphia: Open University Press.

Driver, R., and Bell, B. (1986). Students' thinking and the learning of science: a constructivist view. *School Science Review*, 67, 443–455.

Duckworth, E. (1973). The having of wonderful ideas. In Schwebel, M. and Raph, J. (ed.), *Piaget in the classroom* , New York: Basic Books, pp. 258–277.

Feynman, R. P. (1968). What is science? *The Physics Teacher*, 7(6), 313–320.

2 The Learner

LOOKING AHEAD

In this chapter we will explore what children know before they come into your classroom. As a teacher, you need to be aware of children's concepts of the world for two reasons. First, current learning research indicates that children learn by building new knowledge on top of old. So we have to understand that foundation before we can build the structure. Second, other research has shown that many of the initial impressions children have of science and the world around them are incorrect. Unfortunately, it is very difficult for children to abandon their early ideas.

We also will look at how children think and how their ability to think changes as they mature. You may have run into these topics in an earlier educational psychology class. Here we'll try to apply what researchers have found out about children's thinking and learning directly to the elementary science classroom. For a greater, in-depth discussion about the psychology of children's learning, please consult the general methods text in this series.

CAN YOU?

- Express what children think science is?

- Suggest how childrens' images of science are developed?

- Tell why it is important to be aware of what children already know and how they think about different science topics?

- Discuss what is meant by "learning by construction?"

- Construct a concept map about a specific science topic?

- Discuss what developmental psychology says about how children learn?

WHAT CHILDREN THINK ABOUT SCIENCE AND SCIENTISTS

In school, children quickly discover that science is found in textbooks. "Read chapter six to learn about snakes and do questions 1-6 at the end of the chapter." No wonder children get turned off with science! How much more exciting it would be to find out about snakes by asking one! (Well . . . at least by watching it while it crawls, eats, sheds its skin, and does other "snake-y" things.) Children are very good at looking at things in order to learn from them. If they weren't, all of us would have grown up to be extremely ignorant adults (assuming, of course, that the whole human race wouldn't have died out a long time ago). It is part of our very nature to want to increase our knowledge and understanding of our surroundings. We have evolved as creatures able to adapt to and modify our environment. Unfortunately, nowadays we sometimes concentrate so hard on being teachers that we forget to let the children be the learners they can be.

Children have fairly simplistic images of what a scientist is. Perhaps not too surprisingly, different children's conceptions of scientists are quite consistent. First, children tend to think of scientists as male. Even though women have made important contributions to science and their numbers are increasing, female scientists are mostly overlooked. Children often portray "typical scientists" as quite atypical people. According to children, scientists often have frizzy hair, have evil glares, and display truly menacing laughter (and where do these ideas come from?).

Even though scientists appear to children as potentially unusual individuals, it also seems fairly obvious to children that scientists are very intelligent. You have to be *really* smart to be a scientist. Most "normal" people would not have a scientific career as an option available to them. Scientists somehow "think better than I do." The high intellect of the child's scientist may be tied to the perception of a somewhat unusual personality. This image is reinforced by popular movies showing the mad scientist in his lab. White lab coat, thick glasses, and the frizzy hair are a vital part of the costume.

Perhaps because of the real scientist's extended training and need for a thorough understanding of the field of study, children's imaginary scientists are endowed with essential omnipotent knowledge. They know everything already. Unfortunately, this misses the main point: Scientists realize there are many, many things that they don't understand, but finding out about them can be exciting!

Where do children get their ideas about what science is and what kind of people practice it? It doesn't take much thinking back through movies you've seen to come up with plenty of examples where the stereotypes we've been discussing are reinforced. Has there ever been a monster movie where some mishap of science wasn't at the root of all the troubles on the screen? Television isn't much better. Not many idols of today's children are known for the study habits they model for their fans.

Of course, not all of what children see on television is bad. Public television makes real efforts to display science in a positive light. Many children start out on scientific careers after immersing themselves in the animal shows and other fare broadcast on PBS. Shows like *3-2-1 Contact* help students see that thinking can be fun. Documentaries and flashy shows like *Nova* and *Beakman's World* can get them excited about science. Even *Mr. Wizard* is still around doing his part!

HOW CHILDREN LEARN SCIENCE

As we've discussed, the fact that children's cognitive abilities are still developing has important implications for how we teach them. They have notoriously short attention spans. They can easily become distracted or give up on a problem that stymies them for more than just a few minutes. Making sure that they have plenty of hands-on/minds-on involvement with what they are learning helps ameliorate this problem and also fits in well with the way they learn.

Paradoxically, children at this age are both emotionally fragile and astonishingly resilient! They can be crushed when other children make fun of them or say they are "stupid" because they can't answer a question. But by giving them opportunities to be independent and by helping them to find solutions and admit that there are many things that people don't know, we build confidence and help prepare them for the continual bombardment of problems and decisions that make up adult life. We also can establish in them a lifelong interest in science. We can provide them with the intellectual ammunition needed to evaluate the claims of others and the skills to help them find the answers.

Cognitive Levels

One of the most widely accepted ways of looking at learning was developed by Benjamin Bloom in the 1950s. He and his colleagues categorized levels of understanding into a "taxonomy of the cognitive domain." You are probably already familiar with these six levels, but let's review them again to see how they apply specifically to learning science. It would probably be worthwhile for you to keep Bloom's taxonomy readily available in your memory to help you while teaching and developing classroom materials. If this sounds like a rote memorization task, it is! But sometimes it is a necessary evil. In order to intelligently discuss and explore things, you need the vocabulary. Whenever you (or your students) face such a task, find a way to make it easy. Make up a short song or devise a sentence from the first letters of the words. These mnemonic tricks may seem silly, but they do work. For example, we keep the levels of Bloom's taxonomy in our heads by remembering the sentence: <u>K</u>evin's <u>com</u>puter is an <u>Apple</u> <u>an</u>d it is <u>s</u>imply <u>ev</u>il. This doesn't mean that we don't like Apple computers. The nonsensical sentence just helps us recall the parts of the taxonomy: <u>K</u>nowledge, <u>C</u>omprehension, <u>Ap</u>plication, <u>An</u>alysis, <u>S</u>ynthesis, and <u>E</u>valuation.

Bloom's Taxonomy and Hints to Determine Level

Knowledge: define, list, repeat, name, recall

Comprehension: identify, describe, discuss, express

Application: demonstrate, use, interpret

Analysis: categorize, distinguish, calculate

Synthesis: design, collect, prepare, plan

Evaluation: judge, assess, rate, revise

Let's start with the first level: Knowledge. This is usually taken to mean simple recall. For example, if you can keep your mnemonics straight, you now have a knowledge level grasp of the parts of this taxonomy. You could demonstrate this by simply reciting the names of the different levels. This is certainly not a very demanding criterion for learning, yet it is usually the one teachers and students focus on. No doubt this is due to the fact that this cognitive level is the easiest to evaluate. There can be no doubt about whether a student can recall a simple fact; the student either can or can't.

You are probably already familiar with how Roy G. Biv helps you keep the colors of the rainbow in their proper top-to-bottom sequence. In your science class, you might ask your students to memorize the order of the planets in the solar system. See if you can help them come up with a mnemonic aid. (If you can't recall the correct planetary order, look it up, then *be sure* to devise a good mnemonic!)

The second level of the taxonomy is that of Comprehension. Here the student is able to explain relevant facts about the topic in question. Right now you are building a Comprehension-level understanding of Bloom's taxonomy by reading and thinking about the meaning of the different levels.

Many teachers think they are testing for this level when, in fact, they are just asking for a more thorough memorization. For example, if you asked a sixth grader to label the parts of a flower and describe what they do, that is really a memory task. If you ask for an explanation of how the various parts work together to produce a new flower, you are probably asking for a bit more. Sometimes it's hard to tell a Knowledge-level question from a Comprehension question. Look for words like "discuss," "explain," or "express" rather than "define," "list," or "name." They are the tip-off that you are probably asking for comprehension or understanding of the material.

Application, the next level in the taxonomy, is substantially more difficult for students. It is also quite a lot harder to evaluate. When you as a teacher can come up with an application question, you often hear complaints that "you never covered that." Well, that's exactly the point. If a student understands material at this level, he or she can apply that knowledge to new situations.

The nice thing about teaching at the middle and upper cognitive levels is that they also support learning at the lower levels. If a student really understands a topic well enough to apply it somewhere else, then the individual parts of the topic have meaning, and that meaning makes it easier to recall the material at the Knowledge and Comprehension levels. The facts become part of a network or web of concepts. Each part reinforces the recall of the adjacent section, resulting in easier memorization of the whole.

An example of learning at the Application level might be when students can make a reasonable prediction of the next few days' weather, based on their understanding of meteorology. This works well in class because it is easy to test their predictions—just wait a while!

Once students begin working at the Analysis level, they are beginning to be mature thinkers. Although sometimes hard to find at the elementary school level, a student who can analyze a situation and break it down into more easily understood components is well on the way to the kind of thinking that he or she will need throughout adult life. Certainly this is something to strive for. Most people realize this, but the real challenge is being sure that it is happening. It can be quite difficult to create a valid test of analytic thinking. See if you can come up with a few questions to see if a fifth- or sixth-grade student could approach the ecosystem of a nearby stream or pond from an Analysis level of cognition. Like, "What is the food web of this ecosystem?" "What are the roles (niches) of the different plants and animals that comprise the web?" These are complex questions.

Synthesis-level thinking is the reverse of Analysis. Now we give students different pieces of ideas and ask them to put them together into a grand scheme. This is really the heart of science. Many different observations are combined to lead the scientist toward a testable theory to explain what she or he saw. In the science classroom you will find that as your students pick up more and more of the facts of science, they will be able to put them together to explain new situations or things that you bring to their attention. This is where they will begin to see one of the big paybacks of earlier study. They can take things they already know and rearrange the concepts to help them understand the world around them. If you can get them to this stage by the end of the school year, you will have gone a long way toward promoting an intrinsic motivation to continue their studies in science.

The uppermost cognitive level, at least according to Bloom, is Evaluation. Students never seem to have trouble here. They are more than willing to evaluate any given situation and put their two cents in. That's fine. It is your job to make sure they can justify their opinions. Some of the environmental problems our society faces are excellent starting points. Ask them if paper cups (even wax-covered ones) are always better than plastic. How about using real glasses? To tie these science topics into social studies, have them think about what is driving the current craze to recycle, even though scientists have been telling us to do it for years.

Although our discussion of Bloom's taxonomy has been brief, you can probably see that it is generally (though not always) sequential. In other words, students usually work at a higher level by having gone through all the lower cognitive levels first. The lower levels support thinking at the upper levels. Conversely, upper-level tasks you assign help maintain students' lower-level understanding.

Piagetian Theory

One area of psychological study that definitely has a serial ordering is Piaget's developmental levels. Even though they've been around a long time, Piagetian ideas still have a large influence on our understanding of how children learn. According to studies carried out by Jean Piaget and his colleagues, there are four stages of cognitive development that children go through as they progress from early childhood to adulthood.

Piaget's first stage of cognitive development, the sensorimotor stage, lasts from birth to approximately two years of age. Eventually, children at this stage develop the understanding that objects continue to exist once outside of their visual field. Piaget referred to this as object permanence. Attaining object permanence is important because it signals the early development of memory (among other concepts) in children. Also, children at this level learn strictly through sensory experience of their environment. Toddlers engage in sensorimotor play and experimentation when they eat dirt to better understand and learn about it. As children struggle with their first steps when they learn to walk they are getting a kinesthetic sense of what gravity is all about.

The pre-operational stage, which lasts from the ages of two to about seven, is a period of language development and egocentrism. Children at this stage cannot entertain a perspective other than their own. The child who feels better when holding a particular stuffed animal and offers you the same animal when you are ill believes that "since it works for me it will work for you." Children begin to center —to categorize objects by single, conspicuous features. If a child's Uncle Tim owns a German shepard, the child will refer to every German shepard seen as "Uncle Tim's" dog. Caution should be used when asking the child at this level to classify objects. Pre-operational children cannot effectively cope with multiple classifications. There is a tendency to get classes of objects confused with their subclasses. For example, if you provide a child with 20 black wooden beads, 20 black plastic beads, and 30 white plastic beads and ask, "Do I have more plastic beads or more black beads?" the pre-operational child would indicate that you had more black beads.

During the concrete operations stage, age seven to about twelve, the child begins to acquire the principle of conservation —the ability to understand that an object remains the same even if you make superficial changes to it. Children first acquire conservation of mass. The classic test for this is to show children two balls of clay of equal size. Then roll one of the balls of clay into a cylinder and ask if they are the same, or if the ball has more clay than the cylinder, or if the cylinder has more clay than the ball. A child who has not grasped the idea of conservation might well think that the longer cylinder has more clay in it even though it clearly came from a reshaping of the original ball. For children at the early elementary school level, this mode of thinking is the one most familiar to them. Knowing this in advance helps you plan lessons and hands-on experiences for them that capitalize on their style of thinking.

Conservation of weight is acquired next. Two clay balls are weighed in the presence of the child. Then one ball of clay is reshaped into a cylinder and the child is asked if they weigh the same, or if the cylinder weighs more, or if the ball weighs more. The child who has acquired conservation will realize that nothing was added or taken away from the balls of clay. Therefore, this child will state that they continue to weigh the same.

Finally, the child acquires conservation of volume. One cup of liquid is measured by the child and poured into a tall thin beaker. Another cup of water is measured and poured into a wide shallow dish. The child who has acquired conservation of volume is no longer fooled by these visual tricks. The child realizes that pouring the liquid into different containers did not change the original amount of liquid measured.

Children at the concrete operational stage develop the ability to handle complex logic and to make comparisons. Much more complicated classification schemes can be understood and should be promoted. Nonetheless, children at this developmental level still benefit greatly from hands-on experiences with the subject matter to be learned. Concrete children are able to hypothesize and/or reason abstractly only about those things that they have experienced. Concrete operational children should be provided with a review of the steps involved in solving a problem and should encounter many and varied examples. Piaget (and Jerome Bruner's somewhat different way of looking at development) encouraged discovery or inductive methods of learning. If you can provide your students with a playful trial-and-error way to explore nature, your method will not only fit in well with how the child learns but also promote a positive attitude toward science.

The formal operational stage starts at around age twelve and continues throughout adulthood. Piaget believed that very few individuals ever reached formal operational thinking. Yet, you still might have a few students in the later elementary grades acquiring more abstract thinking capabilities. Children at this stage are no longer bound to the concrete world. However, this doesn't mean that hands-on experience is unnecessary. As a teacher, you can take advantage of the greater mental capabilities of students of this age. What is important for science teaching is that the children's ability to formulate hypotheses, offer interpretations to experiments, and draw conclusions from their experience expands significantly.

Of course, much more could be said about each of these levels and also some of the criticisms of Piaget's approach to developmental psychology. For additional coverage, review the general methods book in this series or find a good educational psychology text. While you are looking up Piagetian theory, look over his ideas on the three types of knowledge: physical, social, and logical. The first deals with a child's kinesthetic senses (learning by performing an action through the senses). The second deals with how the child learns to interact with others. The last is really a sort of mathematical understanding. This knowledge will help you, the teacher, deal with a child's actions while performing a variety of science activities.

Multiple Intelligences

Howard Gardner theorized an extension of Piaget's three types of knowledge. He proposes at least seven distinct kinds of intelligence, including linguistic, musical, logical, spatial, kinesthetic, intrapersonal, and interpersonal. Someone with highly developed linguistic intelligence might be a journalist or author. Musical talents are revealed in fairly obvious ways. Spatial skills are utilized by certain designers and architects —people who are capable of mentally manipulating objects and describing how they change as they rotate or move. Kinesthetic intelligence shows up most commonly as dancing or athletic ability. Intrapersonal intelligence is revealed when a person has a deep understanding of his or her own feelings and inner thoughts. Interpersonal skills mean one gets along well with others, is empathic, and is aware of body language and subtle conversational cues. A well-rounded school should promote development of all these different, fairly independent (according to Gardner) intelligences. In your science classes, consciously strive to incorporate as many different ways of working with the material as you can. Bridging the gap between subjects is getting more and more attention as a way of increasing learning in all areas. For example, writing about what was observed during a field trip not only helps students practice writing skills but is good science, too! This is also an excellent way to reach students who prefer a different mode of learning. Some students learn best by seeing something. Others can learn by just reading about it. Still others need to hear about something before it really makes sense. The more ways you can find to present the material, the more likely any given student will grasp it.

Metacognitive Skills

Knowledge about one's own thinking process is called *metacognition*. There are two types of metacognition: thinking about what we know and thinking about how to learn even more. When you talk about these ideas you are actually teaching your students how to learn. They should consider what they have to learn and how they will know when they have learned it. Something as simple as getting students to ask themselves, "Do I understand what just happened?" can be the start of metacognition. By practicing an "outsider view" of their learning process they can figure out what they still need to know and how long it will take to learn it. Have them think about what learning techniques worked in the past and which ones might be appropriate now. Studies clearly indicate that students practicing metacognitive skills learn better.

Misconceptions Affect What Students Learn

On the first day of school your students already have quite a few ideas about the subjects in your lesson plan for the year. Your students' previous knowledge, whether it is correct and complete or not, may have served them reasonably well all their lives. Now someone comes along and says that the world doesn't work the way they thought. If you were a child, what would you do? Abandon something that is at the very core of how you view the world (and which you can usually verify by simply looking around you) or accept the word of one of the adults, an already suspect group! In Chapter 1 we looked at children's notions of what science is. Later, we will more closely examine preconceptions children have of specific science topics. For now, let's look at a situation where the teacher, knowing in advance some typical misconceptions, brings these naive ideas out into the light for closer inspection.

Mr. Jones: Okay, everyone, watch closely while I toss this ball up in the air. [He throws a small ball vertically about 2 feet and then catches it when it comes back down.] Tell me what happened.

Sam: You threw the ball and then caught it.

Mr. Jones: Can you be more specific? If you were to write a story about what happened, what would you put down first?

Sam: First you had the ball in you hand, then you threw it straight up. It went up and came back down. Then you caught it with the same hand.

Mr. Jones: Why did the ball behave that way?

Sue: Gravity! Gravity makes things fall.

José: But that only says why it fell back down. It went up because Mr. Jones threw it with his hand.

Mr. Jones: Do you remember what we call something that makes things change the way they move?

Several students: A force!

Mr. Jones: Right! Now, what forces were acting on the ball?

Sue: Isn't gravity a force?

Mr. Jones: Does it make the motion of the ball change?

Sue: Yes! So it must be a force. And the other force you did with your hand.

Mr. Jones: Good! Now, when were these forces acting on the ball?

Lee: The force from your hand made it go up and gravity made it come down, but wasn't gravity "on" all the time?

Sandra: Gravity made it stop going up and then made it come down faster and faster. So the motion changed in both places.

Mr. Jones: Right. Now, how about the force from my hand? When is it acting on the ball?

Sam: The force from your hand made it go up, so it worked until gravity made it stop at the top.

Mr. Jones: Could my hand exert a force on the ball after it was on the way up? My hand wasn't touching it anymore. What do you think?

It wasn't until the very end of the discussion that things started going the way Mr. Jones originally had intended. He knew that a common misconception of students is that there must be a force in the direction of motion for any moving object. He tried to set up an event where the students would recall their misconception and then be challenged to examine it more closely. It took a while for that to happen, but it finally did. Now Mr. Jones could spend some time helping the students improve their understanding of the nature of forces and motion. You must be as careful as Mr. Jones when you bring up naive conceptions of science. You don't want to ridicule the ideas because they spring from everyday experience and are part of our common sense. Nonetheless, these ideas have proven to be very resistant to change. When you know some of your students have substantial misunderstandings in a particular area, be sure to meet the challenge head on and sensitively.

Perhaps you won't be surprised to learn that much of the history of science has been involved with debunking people's misconceptions. Galileo's most famous experiment demonstrated that the mass of an object did not determine how fast it fell. It took a long time before people finally rejected Aristotle's idea of tendencies (rocks "want" to fall, flames "want" to rise). Since misconceptions are so common, one of the first things you will want to do when you begin a new unit is to diagnose existing difficulties. Ask your students to discuss or write down what they know about the topic at hand before you start the unit. Ask, too, what questions they have about the topic. Armed with this knowledge, you will have a head start at changing your students' incorrect or incomplete ideas about science.

Besides the ideas they bring with them into the classroom, you must also be aware of the attitude baggage students drag along with them. You may have heard of math anxiety. It's that fear some students display as soon as they find out they need to "do math." They get sweaty palms, their hearts race, and whatever semblance of concentration they had before evaporates! Of course, this causes them to have even less success with math, which reinforces the whole sequence. Unfortunately, math anxiety often also spawns a fear of science. The self-reinforcing cycle works the same way. Be on the lookout for students demonstrating this type of behavior. Encourage them with early successes to build their confidence and positive attitudes toward science and math. Elementary school is the best place to avoid math anxiety and to "immunize" students against future attacks!

Constructivism

Recognizing that students have previous understandings of materials you are trying to teach them isn't so bad. The tough part is that any new knowledge will be filtered by and added to their prior understandings, no matter how confused and incomplete they are! In other words, knowledge accumulates by building on prior experience and understanding. Students construct new ideas by incorporating new material into the concepts and thought processes already in place. In some cases, the fit of new knowledge to old is so poor that the student doesn't even recognize that the new information has any meaning outside the classroom. Difficulty in transferring knowledge to other situations is the result.

The Association for Supervision and Curriculum Development (ASCD) has developed a four-step process for guiding learning through a constructivist-oriented approach. Its model is essentially the problems approach, so let's look at it a bit more closely. In the first stage, learners are engaged by a teacher- or student-generated question. This question may come from a list the teacher has prepared early in the year, from something a student has seen or experienced recently, or even from current events. The ASCD suggests that this is the time to begin recognition of prior understandings and beliefs about the topic. For example, let's say that a recent television show about global warming captured a student's attention. The student could come into class and ask you if the recent warm weather was due to global warming. How would you respond to a question like this? One of the first things to do would be to find out how to find the answer! Perhaps you could find a news magazine that focuses on the problem. You could review it and return to your classroom more informed and ready to offer suggestions on how your students can begin to find the answer. You might want to look at weather patterns over the past several years, perhaps by having your students request information from a local weather station, meteorologist, or airport. You definitely want to spend some time discussing the possible causes of global warming and the greenhouse effect.

Steps Toward a Constructivist Approach to Teaching

- Teacher presents an invitation to learn

- Teacher gives students the opportunity to explore, discover, and create

- Students propose explanations and solutions

- Students take action on what they have learned

In the second stage, you let children discover what they can about global warming. Ask if any of them have ever visited a greenhouse. There might even be one nearby that your class could visit. At the least, a visit to the library should provide information about the major parts of a greenhouse. Perhaps someone will recall how hot their car gets when it is parked in the sun with the windows rolled up. Let them experiment with paper cups of water placed in the sun. Try the effects of different colored water or cups on temperature. What happens when they cover the top of a cup with a plastic bag held on with a rubber band?

The third stage will naturally arise out of the second. Have students talk about how a greenhouse is built and make conjectures as to what makes it work. How does that relate to their hot car or the paper cup with the plastic cover? Before long, they'll begin to see that the key to the greenhouse effect is that sunlight gets in, but heat doesn't easily get out. Now you can start to discuss how carbon dioxide, a waste product from burning fossil fuels, acts as a one-way valve for solar energy. They'll put all the pieces together and come up with a good model for the global greenhouse effect.

Taking action, the last stage, happens when students have integrated the new information with their existing knowledge. Through a combination of exploration, recall of prior experience, library work, hands-on experiences, and prodding from you, the learners will have constructed a new conceptual understanding of the subject. At this point, they may want to write to government officials, local polluters, or scientists working in the area. It isn't much of a stretch to see how this type of activity helps develop informed, scientifically literate citizens.

Brooks (1990) suggests the following approach to constructivist teaching:

- Encourage and accept student autonomy, initiation, and leadership.

- Allow student thinking to drive lessons. Shift content and instructional strategy based on student responses.

- Ask students to elaborate on their responses.

- Allow wait-time after asking questions.

- Encourage students to interact with each other and with you.

- Ask thoughtful, open-ended questions.

- Encourage students to reflect on experiences and predict future outcomes.

- Ask students to articulate their theories about concepts before presenting your understanding of the concepts.

- Look for students' alternate conceptions and design lessons addressing any misconceptions.

To this excellent list, add the following:

- Let students teach each other whenever possible. This forces them to closely examine what they know.

- Encourage other metacognitive activities. Have students think about how they learn. Let them brainstorm to learn even more!

- If you can, have each student or group of students create a tangible product. This gives them a sense of accomplishment and provides something concrete to remember; it forms a base for building additional knowledge.

Concept Mapping

Joseph Novak and Bob Gowin have an excellent book called *Learning How to Learn.* In it they describe their theories about how people build a web or network of concepts. They also suggest that having students build their own map of concepts as they learn about the concepts is a good way to help this process. Concepts are the nodes on the map and relationships between them are illustrated as links. This is not really much different from the constructivist ideas we discussed earlier. Prior knowledge is nothing more than a preexisting map of concepts. Misconceptions are incorrect nodes and/or links. These errors in the map should be diagnosed and corrected to form a stable supporting structure for the addition of new concepts. Here's one example of a concept map:

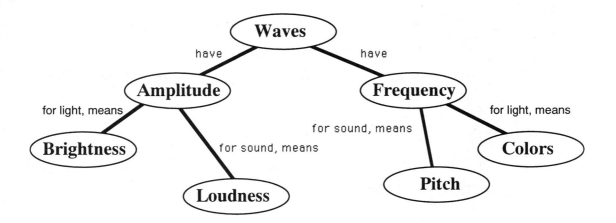

Problem Solving

Children of elementary school age tend to be impulsive and must be taught to take a systematic approach to solving problems. Obviously, the problems approach incorporates problem-solving strategies that will be discussed throughout this book. If you want to focus specifically on problem-solving techniques, take a look at Polya's classic book on problem-solving methodology. Engage your children in games like "20 Questions." They soon learn that careful questioning is necessary if they are to solve the puzzle. Model logical questioning that narrows the possibilities rather than random, trial-and-error guessing.

As a beginning teacher, maybe after an activity is selected and the discrepancy (or problem) is encountered, you might think about focusing important questions as follows:

What is the problem?

What do I already know?

What new information will I need?

What procedures do I need to develop or follow to solve the problem?

How will I communicate the results in a meaningful way?

Asking and answering these questions to creatively solve a problem may involve having students work alone or in small groups, cooperatively working on a solution. More discussion of this important topic is offered in the general methods text of this series.

Learning Styles

There are quite a few models of learning that might be preferred by any one student. These range from sensory orientations (audio, visual, etc.) to social groupings (individual, peers, mentors), to complex psychological possibilities (abstract sequential, reflective observation, and others). Even though these models differ substantially on their approach to the concept of learning styles, they all seem to have similar implications for teachers. First, make sure you don't always teach the same way. (You may have a preferred teaching style that is a poor match for a particular student's preferred learning style.) Second, it is important to help your students identify the ways they learn best. This helps them take some control over how they learn and points the way toward their restructuring information in ways that are more meaningful (or at least more "learnable") to them.

LOOKING BACK

This chapter has provided a very brief review of some of the educational psychology that is relevant to the problems approach to teaching science. Without too much difficulty, you should be able to locate entire books about each area that we covered in a paragraph or two. Investigate two or three. Because our list was by no means exhaustive, there may be other current topics that you might think are important and relevant. Talk to your instructor and other teachers to see how they incorporate the theories of educational psychology into their teaching methodology. Start to plan ways you can do the same.

SELF-TEST

- What do children think science is? How are these images developed?

- Why is it important to be aware of what children already know and how they think about different science topics?

- What are Bloom's taxonomic levels and how do they relate to teaching?

- Discuss Piaget's stages of cognitive development and their importance to science teaching.

- How can a knowledge of students' misconceptions help the science teacher?

- What is meant by "learning by construction?"

- What is a concept map? How can this be a tool for the science teacher?

REFERENCES FROM RESEARCH

Bloom, B. (1968). Learning for mastery. *Evaluation Comment, 1,* 2. Los Angeles: University of California Center for the Study of Evaluation.

Brroks, J. (1990). Teachers and students: constructivists forging new connections. *Educational Leadership,* 47(5), 73–78.

Carroll, J. (1963). A model of school learning. *Teachers College Record,* 64, 723–733.

Clement, J. (1982). Students' preconceptions in introductory mechanics. *American Journal of Physics,* 50(1), 66–71.

Johsua, S. and Dupin, J. J. (1987). Taking into account student conceptions in instructional strategy: an example in physics. *Cognition and Instruction,* 4(2), 117–135.

McCloskey, M., Washburn, A. and Felch, L. (1983). Intuitive physics: the straightdown belief and its origin. *Journal of Experimental Psychology: Learning, Memory, and Cognition,* 9(4), 636–649.

Sharan, S., Kussell, P., Hertz-Lazarowitz, R., Bejarano, Y., Raviv, S. and Sharan, Y. (1984). *Cooperative learning in the classroom: research in desegregated schools.* Hillsdale, N.J.: Erlbaum.

Slavin, R. (1987). Mastery learning reconsidered. *Review of Educational Research,* 57, 175–213.

What research says to the science teacher, volumes 1, 2, 3, 4, National Science Teachers Association, 1742 Connecticut Ave., NW, Washington, DC 20009.

The newsletter *CESI Science* has a column titled "Research in Practice" written by teachers who have first-hand experience at using the findings of educational research in their own elementary and middle school science classrooms. Contact Betty Burchett, 212 Townsend Hall, University of Missouri, Columbus, MO 65211 to find out how to subscribe.

PRACTICAL RESOURCES

3-2-1 CONTACT. Children's Television Workshop, One Lincoln Plaza, New York, NY 10023.

Brown, A. (1978). Knowing when, where, and how to remember: a problem of metacognition. In Glaser, R. (ed.), *Advances in instructional psychology.* Hillsdale, N.J.: Erlbaum.

Driver, R., Guesne, E. and Tiberghien, A. (1985). *Children's ideas in science.* Philadelphia: Open University Press.

Good, R. (1977). *How children learn science.* New York: Macmillan.

Loucks-Horsley, S. (1990). *Elementary school science for the '90s.* Alexandria, Va.: Association for Supervision and Curriculum Development.

National Geographic school bulletin, National Geographic Society, Seventeenth and M Streets, NW, Washington, DC 20036.

National association for research in science teaching, Dr. Glenn Markle, Executive Secretary, University of Cincinnati, 401 Teacher College, Cincinnati, OH 45221.

Needham, R. and Hill, P. (1987). How do children learn? In (ed.), *Teaching strategies for developing understanding in science.* Leeds, England: Center for Studies in Science and Mathematics Education, pp. 2–39.

Newman, D., Griffin, P. and Cole, M. (1989). *The construction zone: working for cognitive change in school.* Cambridge: Cambridge University Press.

Novak J. and Gowan, D. (1984). *Learning how to learn.* New York: Cambridge University.

Polya, G. (1945). *How to solve it.* Princeton, N.J.: Princeton University Press.

School science and mathematics, School Science and Mathematics Association, Lewis House, PO Box 1614, Indiana University of Pennsylvania, Indiana, PA 15701.

Science and children, National Science Teachers Association, 1742 Connecticut Ave., NW, Washington, DC 20009.

Science world, Scholastic Magazines, 902 Sylvan Avenue, Englewood Cliffs, NJ 07632.

The science teacher, National Science Teachers Association, 1742 Connecticut Ave., NW, Washington, DC 20009.

Vygotsky, L. (1962). In Hanfmann, E. and Vakar, G. (trans. and eds.), *Thought and language.* Cambridge: M.I.T. Press.

Vygotsky, L. (1978). In Cole, M. (ed.), *Mind in society: the development of higher psychological processes.* Cambridge: Harvard University Press.

3 The Teacher

LOOKING AHEAD

We all have had teachers who were somehow special. We've also run into people who simply couldn't teach. What is it that makes these people different? Is it possible to learn how to teach or is being able to teach something with which you are born? To be a good teacher you must have empathy—the ability to put yourself into your student's place. You need to view the material that you are teaching from the perspective of someone to whom the ideas are new and possibly confusing. Can this point of view be taught? Yes, some of it can. Educational studies are giving teachers clearer insights into how people think and what influences learning.

By remaining informed by research, paying attention to their own experiences, and adjusting their instruction methods accordingly, good teachers become better and better. Yet, there are still personality traits and interpersonal skills that are probably part of the good teacher's psychological makeup. So why bother with education classes? We like to think of teacher education as very similar to classes at an art school. On the one hand, it makes no sense to attend art classes if you have no natural talent. On the other hand, taking classes will teach the talented budding artist new techniques, expose the artist to the ideas and methods of others, and allow him or her to exploit his or her creativity in new ways. Similarly, education classes, and your methods coursework in particular, can help you build on your own innate teaching talents. You probably recognized some of your teaching ability or you wouldn't have chosen a career in education. Now it is time to learn about what makes the best teachers. We'll begin this task by taking a broad look at methods of teaching, talking about how to organize the classroom and instruction, and outlining different evaluation techniques.

CAN YOU?

- Think of teaching as more a science or an art?

- Think back to one of your favorite teachers. What about that person made him or her different? What attitudes did that teacher instill? What did you learn? How were you taught? What did you like best about that teacher?

- Repeat the second series of questions, only this time, recall one of your least favorite teachers. What makes the difference?

- List and discuss some of the prerequisites to teaching, both from a knowledge standpoint and in terms of personality?

WHY TEACHERS FEAR SCIENCE

Previous Experience

Science is often the one area where elementary school teachers feel inadequate. They may be recalling their own discouraging history of science classes where they feel they somehow managed to sneak by without anyone ever really finding out how little they knew. Or their background might simply be very limited. They know very little science, so how can they be expected to teach it? Besides, if they were really capable of being high-powered science students, they would have just gone on into a scientific career. Doesn't that sound an awful lot like what you read in Chapter 2 about children's attitudes toward science? Not surprisingly, unless taught otherwise, children who are afraid of science grow up to be adults who also distance themselves from the subject. If those adults become elementary school teachers, they can end up instilling the same anxieties into a brand new generation. Either they don't teach science at all or they do it in such a fashion that students soon learn that science is so hard that even their teacher doesn't like it.

As we discussed earlier, adults' dislike of science is really an indictment of current educational practice. If the training of a prospective elementary school teacher included elementary classroom experience where that teacher learned science by just reading it out of a book and then answering the questions at the end of the chapter, no wonder such a teacher is unhappy with the subject! But people often teach as they themselves were taught. Unless they have been exposed to some of the wonder and excitement of science, later on they end up trying to teach science to their students the same unexciting way. But learning disconnected facts that seem to have little connection to the real world is hard, so hard that quite often it doesn't happen. People blame the subject, but it really is the teaching method that is at fault. They come away thinking that science is nothing but a collection of boring, difficult facts, few of which they actually managed to learn.

Teachers Don't Have All the Answers

Luckily, science doesn't require that we know the answers to all the questions that are asked. Nonetheless, this can be frightening to a teacher, especially a new one. Do you show your ignorance by simply saying, "I don't know"? Or do you somehow try to change the subject or pass it off with, "We'll get to that later"? The worst thing to do is to make up an answer, hoping they don't find out. Remember, you are trying to teach, not impress, your students. If you tell them something made up, they might just remember it! Instead, imagine the following scenario:

Johnny: Mr. Smith! Look what Anita found! Isn't it neat?

Anita holds up a 5-cm piece of snake skin for Mr. Smith and the other students now gathered around.

Mr. Smith: What do you think it is?

Anita: It looks like a snake without his insides!

Classmate: Yuck!

Mr. Smith: Where did you find it?

Anita: Me and my friends found it in the stones by the creek.

Mr. Smith: "My friends and I found it."

Anita: Oh, yeah! My friends and I. What is it?

Mr. Smith: Well, it does look like the outside of a snake.

Sally: You mean his skin?

Mr. Smith: Could be. Why don't we plan an investigation of snakes? What should we do?

Anita: Me and Sally . . . I mean . . . Sally and I can go to the encyclopedia and see what it says about snakes.

Johnny: Mr. Smith, can we get a snake to study? We'll take good care of it!

Mr. Smith: Maybe. We'll have to find out what to feed them and how much work it would be . . . how much it costs to buy one, and we'll decide who is going to take care of it.

Johnny: I'll ask my folks to take me to the pet store this weekend. I'll ask there. If it costs too much, maybe we can find one down by the creek.

Mr. Smith: Don't get carried away yet. We need to find out more. Where else can we look for information?

Leo: I think the school library has a book about different kinds of pets. I saw it there a couple days ago.

Sally: We could talk to the people at the zoo to see what they feed their snakes. We can ask them what kinds of snakes are around here, too. We don't want to get a poisonous one!

Mr. Smith: Good idea. Margo, why don't you check that out. Does everybody know what they said they would do, or should we make a list?

Mr. Smith really didn't know much about snakes. He hadn't even thought about poisonous ones until Sally mentioned it. So, in this case, it definitely is a good idea to do a little book work and other research before jumping into the project. There are companies that sell small animals to schools. Try contacting a colleague at a local high school or college for more information on how to purchase and/or care for classroom animals. Pet store owners, too, are very interested in helping teachers. There are lots of things to consider, such as who takes care of it over the holidays and summer? If it were an animal captured nearby, you could probably just return it to its natural surroundings. If it were purchased, you definitely should not release it. It would either die because it is not well-suited to the environment, or it would wreak havoc with the local inhabitants. Perhaps you could give it to a pet store. In any case, your students are sure to learn a lot from closely observing a living thing. But be prepared to wait a while for the snake to shed its skin or the tadpoles to change into frogs. Nature doesn't follow our lesson plans and children can be very impatient.

The main point here is to work together with your students to learn new things together. Don't take the entire burden on yourself, although you certainly need to do some reading and planning.

Be willing to share the work (and the learning and the fun) with your students!

Remember, you don't have all the answers!

In a science workshop with which we were involved, one of the teachers expressed discomfort with not knowing "everything there is to know" about what we wanted our students to learn. We were taking them on nature walks through a creek and meadow area. The students and the teachers would collect samples and record notes in journals. In the classroom, we would work together to try to make sense out of what we'd seen. The teacher felt she was not fully prepared because she didn't always know what sorts of things the students would find. Of course, she couldn't possibly be familiar with every different plant, animal, or rock that the students would bring back, but beyond the need to be aware of certain safety issues—like recognizing poison ivy—it's okay to learn with your students. Model careful and organized observation for them. Show them that curiosity is natural and that learning is fun. Show them how to look for answers to their questions—in the classroom or library. Certainly a little preparatory reading and exploring will help you guide students toward some of the more interesting features—maybe direct them to an area where you suspect some crayfish are hiding. But don't be afraid to learn alongside your students.

Cooperative Learning

You may have already studied cooperative learning. A great deal of research has been done that clearly demonstrates the educational advantages of students working together. Besides the obvious interpersonal skills they develop, it also appears that students often learn more as well as more quickly when grouped together in certain ways. Take a situation where students are working at microcomputers. If a single student at a computer gets stuck and doesn't know what to do next, that student's progress stops. The student will probably sit there staring at the screen or randomly pressing a few keys hoping to hit the right one. But in a group setting, one of the other group members might know of a way around the problem. They can also talk back and forth, bouncing ideas off each other and reinforcing what they are learning. If handled properly, cooperatively working students help each other remember important points and accomplish more than could any single student alone.

There are three ways for students to work in a classroom. The first way is as a single individual. Students learn and are evaluated in isolation from everyone else. They are not dependent on anyone else, except perhaps the teacher. What they know and learn benefits no one but themselves. The second way is for students to compete against each other. This is not usually as much of a problem in elementary school as it is in high school and college, but you should be aware of it. A little competition might be fun for the winners, but watch out for its impact on those who come in last.

The third way, the cooperative model, has students working together. They share the load and so can accomplish more than an individual working alone. There are other benefits, too. In a group discussion, encourage your students to question each other and be able to justify their statements and opinions. Students always seem ready to defend their position. Take advantage of that tendency to encourage higher order thinking. What you want to do is get them to think for themselves.

Children naturally like to work and play together. They are social creatures. This tendency, like their innate curiosity, is often damaged during their years of schooling. They are often penalized when they want to work together. Looking to see what someone else is doing is cheating! Yet cooperation is a fundamental component of the scientific enterprise. You may discover, upon trying to promote cooperative learning the first time in your classroom, that your students are suspicious and just don't know what to do. You need to allay their fears and delineate the different roles they can take when working together. Working with other people will be something that they do their entire lives!

Facing a Challenge to Your Authority

Of course, if you are successful at promoting independent thinking, be prepared for your students to question you as much as they interrogate their classmates. You have to be able to substantiate whatever you tell them. This can be scary if you aren't used to it. If your knowledge of science is a little thin, it can be downright terrifying! Knowing where to find the answers and demonstrating an openness to admit ignorance (which is not being stupid, just uninformed) will help a lot. When you teach a particular science topic for the first time, do some digging for background information beforehand. This will help your confidence, allow you to direct the class better, and make teaching science less frightening. Showing that you are curious to learn an answer will make a bigger impression on the children than you might think!

Perhaps even worse than not knowing the answer is the situation where an elementary school teacher actually does have an excellent grasp of the facts associated with science subjects. There is a very real danger that the teacher puts those facts (or themselves) up on a pedestal. "This is the way it works. Learn it, or else!" The teacher, especially at the elementary level, is looked upon by students as an authority figure, often even above parents. When this person makes a pronouncement about some scientific idea, the best thing to do is to accept and memorize the "truth" that they have bestowed on you. This can make teaching easy—you just stand up in the front, recite the facts, and give them a test when you're done. But it certainly gives an erroneous impression of the nature of science.

With this in mind, what do you think of the following science teaching scenarios?

Mr. Olivere is demonstrating to his fourth graders two different ways to light a light bulb using a battery, a small light bulb, and a wire.

Mr. Olivere: In order for the bulb to light, the bump or bottom end of the bulb has to be connected to one end of the battery and the thread or metal rim of the bulb has to be connected to the opposite end of the battery. The connections may be either by direct contact or through wire. OK, now who can explain what is necessary for a bulb to light?

Fran: The battery has to be connected to the bulb?

Mr. Olivere: OK, one more time [He then goes on to explain again, verbatim.]

Mr. Olivere then passes out drawings showing the four different ways to light the light bulb.

Mr. Olivere: Now let's try this out! Would each group leader pick up a tray that has batteries, bulbs, and wire?

Mr. Olivere: Groups one and two, please do arrangement 1; groups three and four, do arrangement 2; group five, you do number 3; and, group six, do 4 to see that the light bulb in each arrangement will light. Any questions?

Mr. Olivere (after half a second pause): After you finish your experiment, I will ask you to tell me what is connected to what in each of the arrangements.

Compare Mr. Olivere's teaching style to that of Ms. Feinstein who taught the same topic to her fourth graders.

Ms. Feinstein [Distributes class materials (a wire, a small light bulb, and a D-cell battery) by way of class helpers]: I want you to see if you can find four different ways to light the light bulb.

As pairs of students work, Ms. Feinstein circulates and encourages her students to draw their attempts.

Jane: This little hump on the end of the bulb, what does this do, Ms. Feinstein?

Ms. Feinstein: Jason [in the pair next to Jane], can you tell Jane what you found out about that bump on the bulb?

Jason: Look what happens when I do this [connects the bump on the bottom end of the bulb to one end of the battery and the metal rim of the bulb to the other end of the battery]!

Jane: You did it! That bump must be an important connecting point!

Echoing from around the class: We've got it!

Ms. Feinstein: [after a few more minutes of student experimenting] Can we stop now and look up here? [Pause] I want one person from each group to make a drawing of a set-up that worked and put it on the board.

As a class, the students examine their drawings of set-ups. Discussions follow.

Marsha: It looks to me that in order for the bulb to light, the bump on the bottom of the bulb has to be connected to the battery.

John: On one of the ends of the battery.

Leah: And the metal rim of the bulb has to be connected to the opposite end of the battery.

Ms. Feinstein: When all this happens and the bulb lights, does anyone know what this system is called?

Abby: My dad is an electrician and he says that when an electrical fixture doesn't work, it's usually because the circuit is broken and this stops the electricity from flowing.

Ms. Feinstein: Very good, Abby! Now I'd like you to take a look at a sheet of different arrangements of batteries, bulbs, and wires. First, I want you to predict which bulbs will light and then test your predictions.

In the *real* world of science, nature is the authority. People are not. Any statement is subject to close scrutiny. A bit of skepticism is a necessary part of science. The truth is not what someone says, but what nature does. The way to find out if what someone is saying is correct is by examining it very carefully in some kind of controlled situation. In other words, experimentally. Remember what Richard Feynman said? "Science is the belief in the ignorance of experts." For a teacher who is used to being the authority figure in the classroom, doing experiential science can be ego damaging and potentially threatening. It can be scary to let go of the role of "fountain of knowledge." Giving students opportunities to determine what is correct can be very healthy. They will have to do that when they become adults. We might as well give them a chance to practice now!

BATTERIES AND BULBS

Follow Ms. Feinstein's good science teaching example by trying to find out about simple circuits. What is a circuit? It is simply the path of the electrons (electricity) as they move along a conductor (good, common conductors are copper and aluminum). Good Luck!

Title: Batteries and Bulbs

Skills: Observing, recording data, predicting, creating models

Content: Simple circuits, electricity, conductors

Materials: Two 15-cm pieces of bare copper wire (#20), one bulb (#48), one D battery, Simple Circuits Activity Sheet for each team of students

Procedure: Distribute a battery, bulb, and two pieces of wire to each team and have them arrange this equipment in such a way that will make the bulb light. Ask the students if they can find three additional ways to make the bulb light. Ask three or four volunteers to draw a diagram on the board to show the way the bulb lit. Let the students figure out if any of the drawings are really showing the same thing. Hand out the Simple Circuits Activity Sheet and ask the children to predict what will happen to the light bulb in each of the arrangements and complete the questions.

Closure: Ask the students what must be done to make the bulb light. Bring up the concept of a complete circuit during the discussion.

Simple Circuits Activity Sheet

1. Make the bulb light as many different ways as you can using one piece of wire. In the space below, draw all the ways you tried and tell which ones lit and which ones did not.

2. Draw the missing wire(s) in the circuits below. Will the bulbs light the way you have connected each circuit? Construct each circuit to see if the bulb lights.

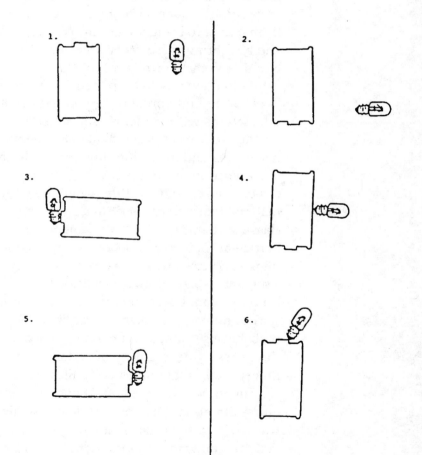

ORGANIZATIONAL PATTERNS

Students at this age seem to enjoy regularly scheduled events. Just like when they sing verses from a repetitious song, children like to know what comes next. As their teacher, you can take advantage of this by setting aside specific times throughout the week to study science. The National Center for Improving Science Education suggests between 120 minutes (for K–3 students) and 300 minutes (for 4–6 graders) per week. As discussed in Chapter 1, always try to be open to questions students bring up about science and the world around them. Strive to bring science into the other subject areas they study and also bring these other areas into the scheduled science time. Nothing in the world is completely isolated from everything else. Why should we try to keep them separate in school?

In addition to organizing your classroom and structuring your interactions with students, you must also consider how you will manage your records and materials. You might want to start a file of newspaper and magazine clippings. Videotapes of parts of interesting science shows (with a written summary of what's on the tape) can be used effectively. When you find or just happen upon science material that you can use (in a store, in your backyard, or in your class), save this material! You might want to keep everything for a particular topic in a shoebox or larger container. That way, everything you'll need will be in one place. Every good science teacher has a separate box (or drawer) set aside to hold "junk." Certainly keep a list of relevant books the children can find in the library. Better yet, start compiling your own science library in your classroom. You will probably also want to maintain your own reference materials so you can refresh your memory of certain areas and come up with new things to talk about or do. Keep files on each specific science topic.

The important question, "How do I set up my room?" also requires attention. Your own style of teaching may dictate that you want to keep the desks in a fairly traditional arrangement of rows. Perhaps you want to stress cooperative learning, so you put groups of four or five desks together. Our favorite arrangement is clusters of four flat-topped desks; two desks facing each other. You now have a team of four students or two teams of two for sharing science ideas and working on activities. Maybe you want to create "science centers" where students can go and easily find all the materials they'll need to explore a particular topic. You also need to consider where to place your classroom computer(s) if you are that fortunate. If you will be displaying the screen to the whole class, put it where all can see it. If you will be assigning students to independent work on the computer, face the screen away from the class and think about whether headphones will be needed. Bulletin board space is always at a premium. Speaking of bulletin boards, can you devise a bulletin board that stimulates thinking, sparks curiosity, succinctly illustrates a complex concept, presents a problem to solve, provides an opportunity to apply learning, captures the essence of a delightful experience, or otherwise brings unforgettable ideas and images into the minds of children? In other words, bulletin boards can be a very important instructional tool! Plan early how you might have your students create a science-oriented display. Contact some publishers and vendors to see if they might have some colorful posters. Talk to your colleagues for their ideas. How about the classroom aquarium and small mammal (we prefer gerbils) set-up? Last, but not least, leave some window sill area free for growing plants.

PLANNING FOR GROUP INSTRUCTION

There is more to setting up a successful group experience than figuring out "how many to count by" when going around the room to assign groups. You may want to be a bit more sophisticated on how you decide who works with whom. Certainly there are times when simple counting off will provide a fast, easy start to a small project. There are other times, however, when you want to have more control over group membership. On the one hand, you might want to consider keeping a quiet child with his or her best friend if that seems like a way to promote that child's active involvement. On the other hand, splitting up a pair of, shall we say, "enthusiastic" children, is often your only way of ensuring that either gets anything done!

Try to balance ability levels in each group. One approach to establishing groups of heterogeneous abilities is to rank order your students from highest to lowest in terms of academic achievement. Rankings are completed privately to avoid student embarrassment. Students are assigned to teams on the basis of rankings: each team includes one high achiever, one low achiever, and two middle achievers. If handled carefully, having a faster, brighter student assist one who doesn't work at quite the same pace can be a positive experience for both. You certainly don't want one child to dominate the group. Nor should you allow any student to sit back and let the others do all the work. You can enforce this best by simply circulating around the room, listening to what's going on. Jump into conversations every now and then to keep the students on track or to suggest an important point they might not have considered yet. If you assign tasks for each individual in the group, rotate them regularly so that each member gets a chance to try each role. Having the best writer always taking notes does that student and the other group members a disservice. In order to make sure each student works to the best of his or her ability, make the group's success dependent on each member's equal participation. There's nothing like a little peer pressure to keep a student on task! Shared responsibility is an important lesson to learn—just as important as the science topic being studied.

Be careful of room arrangements when setting up for hands-on experiences. If the groups will be noisy, make sure they are well separated. If certain groups need access to specific resources, put them within easy reach. Map out a way for you to easily get around the room. You must be able to hop back and forth between groups without disrupting the work going on. It is often a good idea for each small group to report or demonstrate the results of its work to the whole class. Sharing findings is an important component of science. This strategy also is one way to transition from the small group setting back to the larger group.

When the class is working as a whole, you need to have clearly established guidelines for what is expected from each class member. Certainly, the noise level often associated with small groups won't work well when the class is gathered back together. There must be respect for what each person is saying or doing. Since you might want to stimulate debate (or at least discussion) of a particular topic, enforce rules that will help maintain order. You need to decide (before the first day of school) whether students can speak without being called on, how they get your attention, and where and when they can talk among themselves. Classroom rules should be the backbone of defining the behaviors you expect of your students. In fact, rules are a proactive strategy to decreasing problems in a classroom. Discuss rules with the students and why they are important. Elementary school children can be remarkably cooperative when they understand *why* they should do things a certain way. Or better yet, let older children develop the classroom rules. Rules should be worded simply and positively when possible, should describe observable behavior, should be few in number, and should be related to consequences for rule followers and rule abusers. In addition, you might want to establish a special way of getting their attention when you need to. One teacher I know had a little bell on her desk that she would ring when she wanted everyone to be quiet and listen. (Shades of Pavlov and his dog!) Another teacher would flick the lights off and on. A clear-cut rule is easily remembered by students and can work like a charm. The secret is to set up rules and then be consistent in following them.

If you would like to learn more about discipline, take a look in the general methods book that is part of this series.

FITTING TEACHING TECHNIQUE TO MATERIAL

Take advantage of what you have learned about educational psychology. Use some of the tricks of the memory game, showing students mnemonics for things like the color of the rainbow. (You do remember Roy G. Biv, don't you?) You might want to have children shine light through a prism, or even go outside on a sunny day and spray a mist from a garden hose, making a rainbow. The more graphic the lesson, the easier it will be to remember. Sometimes you must get some facts across by standing up in the front, lecturing. This is best done when students have asked you for information; that way, they are automatically motivated to pay attention.

Another, indirect way to introduce science facts to your students is to weave them into the discussion that follows a science activity. For example, in the science teaching vignette about batteries and bulbs, Ms. Feinstein might have introduced the concept of a complete (versus incomplete) circuit just after Abby mentioned "the circuit is broken and this stops the electricity from flowing." The whole class was tuned in at that moment to what makes the bulb light or why it doesn't light. Introducing complete circuits at that time could have been a "teaching moment!"

Occasionally, sound will provide the best technique to demonstrate something from science. If one of your students plays a string instrument, have him or her bring it in. Music is full of science. Let the students feel the vibrations of the instrument as it is plucked or bowed. Have them listen to how the pitch changes when you shorten a string or adjust its tension. Probably the best science teacher in this situation will be the student taking the music lessons! You can provide some of the more scientific vocabulary during or after the demonstration. Maybe the school's music teacher can come in and play a few other instruments so that students can compare how they work and sound.

It is almost always a good idea to ask the students what they know about a particular subject before you really get into studying it. Not only will this help you plan how you want to approach the lessons, it will also point out some of the more interesting ideas children have about the world around them. Some of these ideas, formed through everyday experience, are called misconceptions or, perhaps more politely, naive conceptions. We discussed them briefly in Chapter 2. We will cover them in more detail in the chapters covering specific topics.

After you and the children work on the "What I Know" facts about a topic, brainstorm with your students about "What Questions I Have" about the topic. Each child can do this in his or her own science book (made from folded construction paper). The next section of the science book might be strongly influenced by the local science program: "Observation/Activities To Do" (hands-on activities to find out some answers). Finally, the science book might conclude with a "What I Have Learned" section. Reading, writing, and science are a nice combination!

USING INSTRUCTIONAL MATERIALS

Your choice of how you present a new topic to your students depends on several factors. As we mentioned before, some content areas lend themselves to particular types of materials. It is pretty hard to discuss electricity without letting children have a chance to work with batteries, bulbs, and wires. Similarly, optics without flashlights, mirrors, or lenses can be pretty unexciting. Of course, the overriding factor in your decision is whether you have ready access to materials. Certainly, children love looking at the tiny life forms found in ordinary pond water. But without a microscope or at least magnifying glasses, such a study is quite difficult to carry out. With enough forethought and an understanding principal, you might be able to order equipment or materials. Sometimes you can bring in things that you have at home. (Make sure whatever you bring in is rugged. Although most schools approve of teachers bringing in personal items for class use, few are very excited about replacing those items when they get damaged.)

Probably one of the best ways to incorporate interesting materials into your classes is by having the children bring in their own from home. Egg cartons make great planters for comparing seed growth under different situations. An oatmeal box with holes punched in specific patterns on the end makes a nifty planetarium when a flashlight is placed inside. You can have each child or group make their own constellation and then see if the others can recognize it when it is projected onto the wall. How about having one of the children bring in a family pet (snake, turtle, parrot, hermit crab, or hamster) when appropriate? Of course, you'll need to make sure that science is the topic of investigation (and that none of the children has an animal fur allergy). But with you as a guide, children can learn why snakes shed their skin or what happens to turtles in winter. You can be sure that lessons learned in this kind of actively involving format are not soon forgotten. You might even want to set up a permanent science center in the classroom—with interesting materials brought from home.

Depending on where your school is located, there might be the possibility of exciting science field trips. A zoo or museum is an obvious choice, but don't overlook something as close by as the school play yard or a nearby stream or field. Invite parent chaperones to join you. One of the ideas we want to get across to the children is that science is all around them. Why not show them? If you can't take the children out to the science, maybe you can bring it in to them. You'd be surprised at how many science professionals (sometimes parents) would be willing to visit your classroom and talk to your students about their job and how they "do science."

From earlier discussions, you may have gotten the idea that we don't think textbooks have any place in the classroom. This isn't true. As pointed out before, textbooks should not be a child's only exposure to science. They can be a vital supplement to guided observations. They organize facts and often have excellent photographs or drawings of things that can't easily be seen in the classroom. By all means, take advantage of that! The greater the number of ways you can present information to students, the better the chance that you'll hit just the right way to sneak the material into their heads. (So not only is that the argument for including textbook work in your science lesson but also the reason why you don't want to rely exclusively on books.) Some students might subscribe to some of the newer science magazines that are now being published for children. If so, have them share them with the class, or even order them for the library. You can find addresses for several of them at the end of this chapter.

If you have access to a computer in your classroom (possibly hooked up to an overhead projection tablet), you can run all sorts of fun science software. Perhaps your students will get the chance to operate a nuclear power plant or experiment with animal breeding. When the real thing can't be done in the classroom, a simulation on the computer lets students see the major points without most of the difficulties like radiation, expense, or time constraints. Computer software has come a long way from simple drill and practice—electronic flashcards. For example, you can take a "computer field trip" to a lake and investigate the food chains/web of the lake by using the MECC program "Odell Lake." Videodiscs, too, can bring practically anything you want into your classroom.

EVALUATING SCIENCE LEARNING

It has been said that tests drive the curriculum. What does this mean? In most cases, it is meant to be derogatory. Rather than letting the topics and their interrelationships determine what is taught and how it is covered, our instruction is shaped to a large extent by how we plan to evaluate student learning. This may or may not be the case, but it certainly cannot be denied that testing strongly influences student learning! It doesn't take much teaching experience before one gets tired of hearing, "Is this gonna be on the test?" This may not be as severe a problem in the early grades as it is in high school and college, but it indicates student concern with grading and evaluation, nonetheless.

One way to combat this preoccupation with evaluation is to give the students the responsibility for it! If they know exactly what they have to do to earn a particular grade, the entire process becomes less mysterious and certainly more attainable. It also removes a lot of the subjective judgments required of teachers.

Try and use hands-on assessment and try to make it fun. An interesting part of a hands-on test developed at the University at Buffalo (New York) has students trying to discover the pattern of aluminum foil that connects holes in cardboard. By connecting a battery, bulb, and wires between different pairs of holes, they try to determine the shape of the foil between two sheets of cardboard.

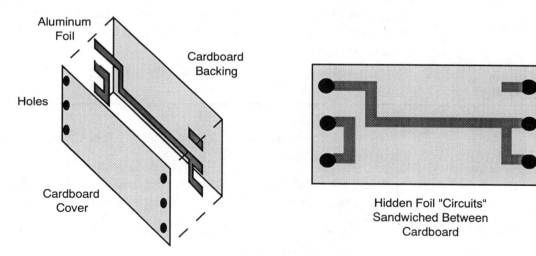

Aluminum Foil

Cardboard Backing

Holes

Cardboard Cover

Hidden Foil "Circuits" Sandwiched Between Cardboard

You can make up several different circuits, let your students work on them for a set period of time, and then let the students take them apart to see if they were right. In other words, the students learn while taking the test. Now, there's a novel idea! (Don't take this to extremes though. Children need to feel free to explore and investigate something without always wondering if they will somehow jeopardize their science grade if they don't find the answer.)

Another example of performance based assessment, this time at the kindergarten level, would be to allow the child to observe two objects—a marble and a square wooden block. Ask the child, "What is one way the two objects are different?" (If possible, record the student responses.) Then ask, "What is another way the two objects are different?" (Again, record the responses.) You can setup your own simple scoring system and really gain an insight of how different children are performing in science. Most important, too, the children actually enjoy this type of hands-on assessment.

LOOKING BACK

In this chapter, we have looked at what it takes to be a science teacher. It mostly boils down to an openness to try new ideas, a willingness to follow student questions, and a curiosity to seek out answers to interesting situations. You not only need to have materials organized for ready access and plans on hand for presenting exciting situations for study, you must also be prepared to be an example of an interested learner.

SELF-TEST

- Why do some elementary school teachers feel uneasy about teaching science?

- Discuss the following statement: In order to teach about a specific subject, one must know something about that subject matter.

- Compare Mr. Olivere's and Ms. Feinstein's teaching of Batteries and Bulbs. Which science teacher do you relate to most favorably and least favorably? Why?

- It's a month before you begin your first teaching assignment. You're spending the day in your fourth grade classroom to get organized. What will your day be like?

- Now it's the first day of class, what rules and guidelines have you established to launch the new school year for you and your students?

REFERENCES FROM RESEARCH

Hewson, P. and Hewson, M. (1988). An appropriate conception of teaching science: a view from studies of science learning. *Science Education*, 72(5), 597–614.

Maheady, L., Harper, G., Sacca, K. and Mallette, B. (1991). *Classwide student tutoring teams: instructor's Manual.* Fredonia, N. Y.: SUNY College at Fredonia.

Rhode, G., Jenson, W., and Reairs, H. (1992). *The tough kid food: practical classroom management strategies.* Longmont, Colo.: Sopris West, Inc.

Rowe, M. (1974). Wait-time and rewards as instructional variables, their influence on language, logic and fate control: part one—wait time. *Journal of Research in Science Teaching*, 11, 263–279.

Tobin, K. (1984). Effects of extended wait time on discourse characteristics and achievement in middle school grades. *Journal of Research in Science Teaching*, 21(8), 779–791.

Willett, J. B. and Yamashita, J. J. M. (1983). A meta-analysis of instructional systems applied in science teaching. *Journal of Research in Science Teaching*, 20(5), 405–417.

Wise, K. C. and Okey, J. R. (1983). A meta-analysis of the effects of various science teaching strategies on achievement. *Journal of Research in Science Teaching*, 20(5), 419–435.

PRACTICAL RESOURCES

Doran, R. (1980). *Basic measurement and evaluation of science instruction.* Washington, D.C.: National Science Teachers Association.

Gentile, R. (1984). *Motions, emotions, and commotions: social learning at home and in the classroom.* Dubuque, Iowa: Kendall/Hunt.

Kids Discover, PO Box 54205, Boulder, CO 80322-4205.

MECC (Minnesota Education Computing Consortium), 6160 Summit Drive North, Minneapolis, MN 55430-4003, 1-800-685-MECC.

National Geographic Explorer, National Geographic Society, Seventeenth and M Streets, NW, Washington, DC 20036.

Ranger Rick, National Wildlife Federation, 1400 16th Street, NW Washington, DC 20036, 1-800-432-6564.

ZooBooks, PO Box 85384, San Diego, CA 92186.

4 The Science Program

LOOKING AHEAD

You may have gotten the impression from earlier chapters that all you have to do is walk into the classroom and wait for children to ask questions and then start science investigations. Your preparation would just involve knowing where to find information to answer those questions and where to get materials to allow for hands-on exploration to find answers to questions. Actually, that is only partly correct. Certainly you need to be flexible and responsive to the children's interests. That is vital and makes science fun for both student and teacher. Nonetheless, it is equally important to provide children with a structured program that endeavors to cover the major topics of science in a coherent manner. This requires planning on a larger scale, not just considering what to teach tomorrow or this week or even this year. The best science programs have come about by careful planning how each grade level's instruction fits together to form a comprehensive program of study. Individual teachers can't really carry out such planning by themselves. They need to work cooperatively with their colleagues in the school so that they don't overlap (except where intended) or miss important science concepts, skills, and attitudes.

Of course, this group planning can generate its own difficulties. Get two science teachers into a room and you will find two different approaches to teaching science. More often than not, you'll also overhear a debate over which program or system is best. This chapter attempts to clarify some of the issues involved in designing your own science program—whether you create it from scratch or closely follow a package made available by a publisher. We will be looking at some things you need to work out for yourself and other things that are best worked out with other teachers and the principal or science supervisor.

CAN YOU?

- Think which of the following is most important in elementary science teaching: the content of science, the processes (or skills) of science, or students' positive attitudes toward science?

- Discuss what features make a good science program?

- Suggest those common features that all science programs should have?

- List the components you will incorporate into your own science program?

- Discuss how you will design such a science program and how will you ensure that it integrates other subject areas?

SOME SCIENCE PROGRAM PHILOSOPHIES

When developing a philosophy of how we want to teach, one place we have to be careful is in the comparison of different ideas. Many logical straw men have been brought into discussions to provide easy targets to tear down. Perhaps by contrasting the extremes of some of the more common debates, you will begin to see that the best course is usually one of moderation.

The all-or-nothing argument: "You either teach them the important facts or they don't learn anything. There's too much fluff in today's curriculum. I've got a lot more experience than children, and I can present science topics to them more efficiently than they can discover these things for themselves."

As is true in most debates, there is some truth in these arguments, which are sometimes couched in back-to-basics rhetoric. There is an important body of knowledge that children must learn, just to survive as adults in today's world. There is no denying that the teacher has been around a lot longer than his or her students. It certainly might be more time efficient to hand students lists of facts to be memorized. But the question that remains is, "Will there be greater retention and understanding of the material?" It appears that in science, as in many other areas, less is more. In other words, covering fewer topics—but in greater depth—results in better learning than a cursory overview of many unrelated concepts. It is vitally important to provide a clear picture of how the different topics of science fit together.

The content-driven versus open-ended curriculum argument: "By sticking with an outline of important topics to cover, thorough coverage is ensured. An open-ended approach will almost always miss some of the central facts and principles."

This strict content-oriented philosophy is often tied to the all-or-nothing argument, mostly from an efficiency standpoint. What people need to think about is their definition of *efficient*. If they are considering efficiency of teaching, there is no debate—they win! However, efficiency of learning and retention is another story. Research indicates that children construct their own meanings for concepts. When instruction is designed around this realization, students learn and remember more. When children are given an opportunity to be creative in their approach to learning science, they tend to be more highly motivated and can often find a better fit to their personal style of learning, especially if they've been taught metacognitive strategies. Although a well-thought-out plan is of prime importance, flexibility and a willingness to address questions of interest to children is also critical. (Remember the "Questions I Have" section of the student science book from the last chapter?) Of course, a curriculum that does nothing but follow the whims of the students actually does them a disservice. They do need to learn the central concepts of any given area of study. But, a curriculum that is so bound to the syllabus that student interests are ignored (i.e., discouraged) might enable the teacher to impart those facts that have been selected as important, but also decreases the chances that the students will ever be interested in learning anything else about the subject!

The textbook/worksheet orientation versus free for all labs argument: "We don't have the equipment or time for hands-on experiments. Besides, it's a waste of time and effort. The children really don't do anything other than play. What if they don't learn the concepts I want them to?"

These are often the arguments of teachers who are unsure of their own science knowledge. The real concern is what to do when something happens that they can't explain. Following the textbook seems much safer. It is important to remember that there is no way that you can know the answer to every possible experimental problem or question that arises. There are too many things that can happen! Instead of trying to be the fountain of knowledge, transfer some of the responsibility for finding the answers to your students. Also, let them design some of the apparatus and experiments themselves from everyday materials. This will quickly get them involved in science and it reduces the impression that scientific instruments are expensive things kept in the cupboard at school, not to be used (or having any use) outside the classroom. The kind of thinking skills that are encouraged by designing, carrying out, and analyzing experiments are central to science and many other endeavors. Research shows that experimenting skills are closely related to formal thinking abilities. We cannot expect students to do well at skills they have not practiced repeatedly. These basic skills can be taught and readily transferred to new situations.

The content versus process versus attitudes argument: Probably the biggest debate has been among proponents of these three schools of thought. We've already discussed some of the concerns of the content orientation. Other people feel that, at least at the elementary level, time learning specific facts is misspent. Instead, they suggest a focus on the processes or skills of science. Children need to learn how to measure distances and temperatures, isolate and control variables in science experiments, and generally attend to "how science is done." The last group feels that what really counts at this age is not science facts or skills, but the development of positive feelings toward science. If all you can do is get children to like science, you will have reached your goal. As you probably expect, a combination of these ideas appears to be the most appropriate. By developing a program that stresses important facts and skills (reinforced by extensive hands-on experiences) you also have the best chance of creating positive feelings about science. Whether you expose children to new ideas first and then have them explore or do the reverse is up to you. Try both methods and see which works better and under what circumstances.

IS THERE A *BEST* APPROACH?

With all these conflicting philosophies, is there really any hope of your coming up with a style and program of your own? Each of the extreme points of view has arguments in its favor. Your own program will probably be some combination of parts of all these philosophies. The program you develop will be different than anyone else's. But are there things that different science programs should have in common? Research in classrooms has identified key instructional strategies to help students overcome their naive, inappropriate conceptions and construct strong, correct ideas about science. If teachers, each following different approaches and programs, keep these in mind, their students will be the beneficiaries.

Research indicates that teachers should:

• Diagnose students' thoughts about the topic and help them to clarify what they think.

• Provide a direct contrast between students' views and the desired view, leading students to be dissatisfied with their existing, inappropriate ideas.

• Provide hands-on opportunities to use the desired view to explain a phenomenon, making it more plausible.

Commercially Available Curriculum Packages

One way to go about developing your own science program is by looking at program packages that have been put together by others. In the 1960s, largely as a national response to the Soviet satellite Sputnik's launch (1957), many groups tried new approaches to teaching science. By briefly examining several of the most popular of these, you might pick up some ideas you can use in your own program. We'll start with Science–A Process Approach (SAPA). As you can guess from its name, it is strongly oriented toward developing the skills of science. (Some have criticized this program, perhaps unreasonably, for downplaying content.) The materials were developed by making observations of working scientists and breaking down what they did into sequences that could be learned by children. Each grade level had about 20 activities. SAPA II, the latest version, has been restructured to allow more teacher flexibility in designing instruction.

SAPA's Basic (K-3) Science Process Skills

- Observe: use the senses to collect data

- Infer: make an educated guess about an event or object

- Measure: use an instrument to collect data

- Communicate: use words or pictures in a description

- Classify: group or order objects or events in categories

- Predict: form expectations of future events from a pattern found in data

---

SAPA's Integrated (4-6) Science Process Skills

- Control variables: isolate and make constant those parameters that might affect the outcome of an experiment

- Operationally define variables: conceptualize variables by how they might be measured in an experiment.

- Formulate hypotheses: predict an experimental outcome

- Interpret data: organize data and draw conclusions

- Experiment: include questioning, hypothesizing, identifying, controlling, and operationally defining variables, designing, conducting, and interpreting results of an experiment

---

The Science Curriculum Improvement Study (SCIS) focuses on depth rather than breadth. There are 12 units in this K-6 program, each dealing with a central concept or big idea in science. Each of these units has several parts and carefully integrates process skills with content learning. In the SCIS learning cycle, children generally have some kind of hands-on activity (exploration) before discussing any abstract concepts (invention). Later, children apply what they have learned previously to new situations (discovery). This is similar to the problems approach this book suggests, although it is not as open to what children might bring up and doesn't stress the importance of teachers diagnosing prior knowledge. SCIS II and SCIS III have been restructured and updated.

The SCIS Program

LEVEL	LIFE SCIENCE	PHYSICAL SCIENCE
1	**ORGANISMS** organism habitat birth food web death detritus	**MATERIAL OBJECTS** object serial ordering property change material evidence
2	**LIFE CYCLE** growth generation development biotic potential life cycle plant & animal genetic identity metamorphosis	**INTERACTION & SYSTEMS** interaction evidence of interaction system interaction at a distance
3	**POPULATIONS** population plant eater predator animal eater prey food chain community food web	**SUBSYSTEMS & VARIABLES** subsystem solution histogram variable evaporation
4	**ENVIRONMENTS** environment range environmental factor optimum range	**RELATIVE POSITION & MOTION** rectangular reference object coordinate polar coordinate relative position relative motion
5	**COMMUNITIES** producer community consumer food transfer decomposer raw materials photosynthesis	**ENERGY SYSTEMS** energy transfer energy source energy chain energy receiver
6	**ECOSYSTEMS** ecosystem water cycle oxygen—carbon-dioxide cycle pollutant food-mineral cycle	**MODELS: ELECTRIC & MAGNETIC** scientific model electricity magnetic field

---

SCIS Lesson Phases

- Exploration: hands-on activities to examine new ideas

- Invention: students and teachers discuss what they are learning; the teacher imparts new vocabulary

- Discovery: additional experiences to extend and reinforce concepts and skills

---

The Elementary Science Study (ESS) was also developed as part of the nation's response to the launching of Sputnik. There are 41 relatively self-contained units dealing with a wide variety of content areas. Teachers (or schools or districts) decide which sets of materials to use. All of the units stress personal involvement: "The child must work with his own hands, mind, and heart." Many of the tasks are open ended and encourage creativity. As children "mess about" with different, interesting materials they are motivated to ask great questions and find their own answers. It is a very teacher- flexible program!

ESS Program Units and Grade Levels

Growing seeds (K-3)	Colored solutions (3-8)	Match and measure (K-3)
Whistles & strings (4-5)	Mobiles (K-4)	Bones (4-6)
Primary balancing (K-4)	Small things (4-6)	Pattern blocks (K-6)
Earthworms (4-6)	Geo blocks (K-6)	Peas and particles (4-6)
Eggs and tadpoles (K-6)	Batteries and bulbs (4-6)	Tangrams (K-8)
Optics (4-6)	Attribute games and problems (K-9)	Pendulums (4-6)
Spinning tables (1,2)	Microgardening (4-7)	Brine shrimp (1-4)
Senior balancing (4-8)	Printing (1-6)	Behavior of mealworms (4-8)
Structures (2-6)	Stream tables (4-9)	Sink or float (2-7)
Water flow (5-7)	Clay boats (2-8)	Mapping (5-7)
Drops, streams, and containers (3-4)	Heating & cooling (5-7)	Mystery powders (3-4)
Balloons and gases (5-8)	Ice cubes (3-5)	Gases and airs (5-8)
Rocks and charts (3-6)	Kitchen physics (6-7)	

PROGRAMS OF THE 90's

Don't think that now that the United States has won the space race, whatever that might mean, that science curriculum development has come to a halt. There are still many groups working hard at improving how science is taught. Today, a number of new programs have become available to elementary science teachers. These new programs retain many of the strong features of the post-Sputnik programs, build onto others, and introduce new features, including the following:

- topics and activities that have far more personal and social applications;

- integration of more subjects, particularly language arts;

- activities challenging students' misconceptions and allowing time for students to rethink their own ideas and schemata;

- teachers and administrators having more say in the design of the programs, and;

- more prominently featured ways to help teachers teach the program and manage the materials.

A short description of each of these new, exciting programs of the 90s follows.

Science Programs

The Biological Science Curriculum Study (BSCS) elementary science program was developed for students in grades 1 to 6. It is not just biology. "Science for Living: Integrating Science, Technology, and Health" allows children to build their own understanding of an integrated world of science, technology, and health as they work through activities that bring out various concepts and skills. Each grade level has a special theme: order and organization (grade 1), change and measurement (grade 2), patterns and prediction (grade 3), systems and analysis (grade 4), transformation and investigation (grade 5), and balance and decisions (grade 6). Each lesson has the following five parts:

1. Engagement: students connect to previous knowledge (and misconceptions)

2. Exploration: students participate in hands-on activities to examine new ideas

3. Explanation: students discuss what they are learning; teacher describes learning objective

4. Elaboration: students participate in additional activities to increase understanding

5. Evaluation: students and teacher assess what has been learned

The Full Option Science System (FOSS) is a new program designed to serve both regular and special education students in a wide cross section of schools. Sixteen modules, four at each grade level, include science lesson plans in the earth, life, and physical sciences, and extension activities in language, computer, and mathematics applications. Nine of the SAVI/SELPH (Science Activities for the Visually Impaired/Science Enrichment Learning for the Physically Handicapped) modules are the starting points for FOSS modules.

Much care is taken to have a suitable match between activities and students' ability to think at different ages. Further work has been done to make the program easy to instruct and manage. Provisions for preparation time, ease of giving out and retrieving materials, cleanup, storage, and resupply have continually guided program developers.

Improving Urban Elementary Science (Insights) is a new program that targets urban schools and city school children. It contains 24 activity-based modules that can be used separately within another science curriculum or as a full curriculum within the life, earth, and physical sciences. Activities, often open ended, focus on experiences that draw on the urban environment and that interest city children. Content and process skills are balanced across the curriculum. Material from other school subjects is integrated into many activities to give an overall understanding of how they normally relate. Instructional materials are designed for both the inexperienced teacher and the veteran who seeks innovative strategies to develop critical and creative thinking in urban students.

The National Geographic Kids Network has children gather data on real science problems and then use a computer network to share their data with a scientist and children in other locations. The developer is the Technical Education Resource Center (TERC) in partnership with the National Geographic Society, which publishes and distributes the program. Each of the instructional units is six weeks long and focuses on a central science problem. Children learn to ask questions and gather data in scientifically acceptable ways. The data are transmitted to an interested scientist who analyzes the data, answers children's questions, and then sends back an overview of all the collected information from cooperating schools. There are currently seven units that make up the program: Hello, Acid Rain, Weather in Action, What are We Eating?, Too Much Trash, What's in Our Water?, and Solar Energy.

The Life Lab Science Program is a comprehensive elementary science program founded on its successful garden-based science curriculum, The Growing Classroom. The Living Laboratory, Life Lab's main component, offers a rich context for exploring science. It consists of an indoor center and an outdoor garden area, which can be as simple as a planter box or as complex as an acre farm. In creating an environment, students learn processes and concepts vital in the exploration of the natural world. At the same time, the garden gives them an opportunity to positively affect their surroundings. In short, there's a lot of growing going on!

The Science Connection: Science Classroom Mini-Museums consists of hands-on kits, featuring unique and interesting manipulatives. The independent-learning format of the kits makes them like interactive exhibits in a museum. The Houston Museum of Science provides constructive plans for 15 interactive exhibits per grade level. Construction kits include all activity cards and cardstock manipulatives for each exhibit as well as blackline masters for student worksheets. Teachers can decide if they want to construct just one exhibit to use in a learning center, to build 15 different exhibits to set up as a mini-museum in the classroom, or to make multiple copies of specific activities for hands-on work in cooperative groups.

Super Science: A Mass Media Program, a colorful, new, year-long, hands-on classroom science magazine, is published by Scholastic, Inc. Eight monthly issues enrich the science curriculum with easy-to-do life, earth, and physical science activities and science news, all integrated with language arts and social studies. The Blue Edition of *Super Science* is for grades 4 through 6 and the Red Edition is appropriate for grades 1 through 3. Each colorful issue focuses on one theme and approaches it from several different perspectives, using familiar examples, to give students a unique experience coupled with thorough comprehension.

And More Science Programs!

The National Science Resources Center in Washington has put together a resource guide for elementary science teachers that is being published by the National Academy Press. They also have been working on 24 science units on Science and Technology for Children. Each unit (there are four per grade level, grades 1-6) emphasizes a different, age-appropriate topic in the life, earth, and physical sciences and technology while developing children's critical thinking and problem-solving skills. They are available from Carolina Biological Supply.

The Technical Education Research Center in Cambridge, Massachusetts, has been developing a large assortment of high-tech, high-touch materials for use at all age levels. Besides the development of the National Geographic materials noted earlier, they also publish an excellent newsletter called "Hands On!" and have taken the lead in the development on microcomputer-based laboratory materials for teaching science and mathematics. One of their projects resulted in a series of lessons that allow children to telecommunicate with other students around the country. Not only are there interesting science packages (which might have students collect data on the acidity of their rainwater for comparison with data collected by children in other states), but there are also nice mathematics lessons as well. (For example, "What is the average allowance for fourth graders, nationwide? Is one area higher than another?" "How much does age affect size of allowance?" Important research questions for children!)

Great Explorations in Math and Science (GEMS), a wonderful, new, flexible, integrated math and science curriculum, comes to us from the Lawrence Hall of Science (Berkeley, California). There are about thirty-three GEMS units that range from "Animal Defenses" and "Buzzing a Hive" to "Global Warming and the Greenhouse Effect." Each unit includes a teacher's guide of activities that provides detailed information on the materials needed for the unit, as well as how to prepare for each activity. From a chemical reaction in a Ziploc bag to the blowing of giant bubbles, from a strange green substance said to come from outer space to hands-on experiments in solar heating, the goal of each GEMS activity is to captivate the child's imagination while illuminating essential scientific concepts and developing inquiry skills needed in everyday life.

Activities that Integrate Math and Science (AIMS) is a series (grades K-1; 2; 3-4; 5-9) of books (actually a collection of activities for children) that give children real-life experience in mathematics and science. The emphasis of the program is to integrate mathematics and science in a realistic manner and in ways that are naturally stimulating and meaningful. From *Fall into Math and Science* to *Fun with Foods*, each AIMS book offers approximately 20 hands-on investigations that often include related language arts and social studies activities. Kits of materials are available for each series, but materials also can be purchased locally.

Project 2061 of the American Association for the Advancement of Science (AAAS) is not really a curriculum program, but does outline six themes that the AAAS felt should be familiar to all Americans: systems, models (both physical and mathematical), constancy (stability, equilibrium, conservation, and symmetry), patterns of change (trends, cycles, and chaos), evolution (possibilities, rates, interactions), and scale (intuitive understanding of relative comparisons). Other groups follow similar ideas, suggesting the use of major themes or concepts as the foundation of a curriculum that emphasizes a meaningful overview rather than meaningless, isolated facts (properly called "trivia"). Although you can organize your own curriculum (which is a very large task!) around specific topics you've found to be exciting to children or perhaps around some processes or attitudes you'd like to develop in your students, it can't be emphasized enough that you need to pick out themes that interconnect the different concepts and help students build a framework for further understanding. Out-of-context facts (like those often presented on vocabulary worksheets) are usually meaningless and not remembered much after the test.

If you have access to a videotape player, you might want to consider one of the two *Voyage of the Mimi* packages developed by the Bank Street College of Education. The *Mimi* is a research sailing ship with a crew of scientists and children. Many exciting adventures are portrayed in 15-minute video episodes. These are supplemented by video visits to places where "real" science is carried out. There are teacher and student guides, microcomputer-based laboratories, computer software, and other materials. Students not only learn science but also see that science is something they can do. They become involved with stories where scientists are actually role models.

A videodisc player opens up many additional possibilities. One of the more extensive series of video-based science lessons is available from Optical Data Corporation. Their Windows on Science packages cover earth science, life science, and physical science. The materials also include a Resource Binder of lesson plans and unit summaries. The Space Disc packages include the *Voyager Gallery, Planetscapes,* and *Space Shuttle* videodiscs. There are numerous, good videodisc packages on the market. Lists of available products can be found in the catalogs of some of the companies listed at the end of this chapter.

There is a wealth of curriculum materials out there from which to choose. Probably, the school or district where you teach will already have a science program in place. Don't be upset if it is not your favorite one, there is flexibility within all of these curricula to make room for a most important person in the curriculum—you!—your style and favorite lessons.

TYPICAL SCOPE AND SEQUENCE OF SCIENCE PROGRAMS

You will often hear discussions of scope and sequence issues during curriculum development. Exactly what do these terms mean? Simply stated, *scope* deals with *what* is covered. *Sequence* is concerned with *when* it is taught. There is fairly good agreement on what topics and skills are important. Unfortunately, there is no such generally approved list of when these things should be taught. In fact, there also is debate on whether certain topics should be covered at every grade level (in greater detail each year), repeated every few years in an effort to improve retention, or covered only once. The trend is away from repetition, but this is by no means universal. Many of today's programs suggest visiting each topic once while stressing how the topics fit into broad conceptual schemes (for example, "living things," "matter and energy," and "earth and space"), which are seen over and over.

You can be almost certain that your school district or state has already put together some form of plan or program for elementary science instruction. To help you see what sort of information is contained in such a document, look over the following example of a state plan—the plan from New York State's Elementary Science Syllabus. It is based on four important science program areas: content, attitudes, skills, and problem solving. Each area has a corresponding goal that supports the overall syllabus goal.

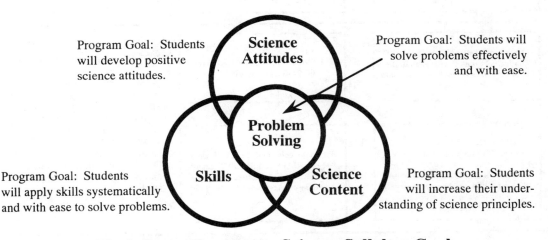

Program Goal: Students will develop positive science attitudes.

Science Attitudes

Program Goal: Students will solve problems effectively and with ease.

Problem Solving

Program Goal: Students will apply skills systematically and with ease to solve problems.

Skills

Science Content

Program Goal: Students will increase their understanding of science principles.

**New York State Elementary Science Syllabus Goal:
Students will demonstrate an increase in their scientific literacy.**

The principles in the Science Content component of the New York State Elementary Science Syllabus are organized in the following general scope and sequence scheme. The principles have been organized into two broad categories: Life Science and Physical Science. The statement, "The natural world consists of living and nonliving objects, and the events in which they are involved," is both the beginning of and the foundation for the entire science content scheme. The scope of the science content includes the major principles that you should include in your science program. The se-

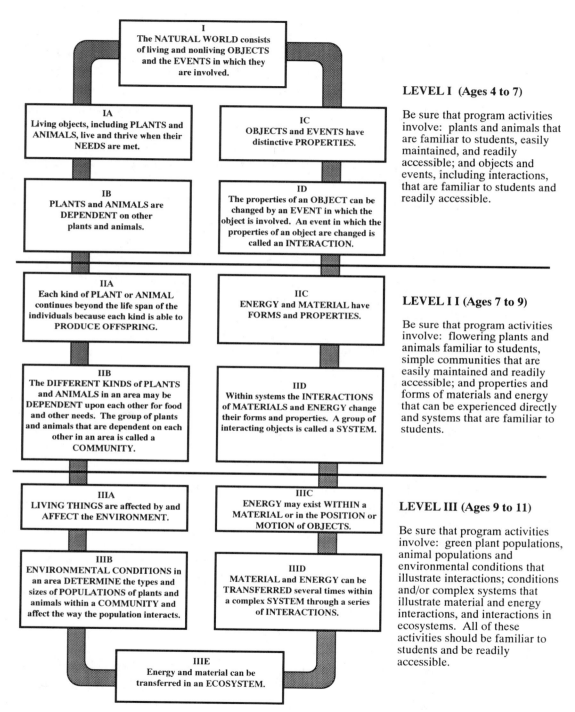

I
The NATURAL WORLD consists of living and nonliving OBJECTS and the EVENTS in which they are involved.

IA
Living objects, including PLANTS and ANIMALS, live and thrive when their NEEDS are met.

IC
OBJECTS and EVENTS have distinctive PROPERTIES.

IB
PLANTS and ANIMALS are DEPENDENT on other plants and animals.

ID
The properties of an OBJECT can be changed by an EVENT in which the object is involved. An event in which the properties of an object are changed is called an INTERACTION.

IIA
Each kind of PLANT or ANIMAL continues beyond the life span of the individuals because each kind is able to PRODUCE OFFSPRING.

IIC
ENERGY and MATERIAL have FORMS and PROPERTIES.

IIB
The DIFFERENT KINDS of PLANTS and ANIMALS in an area may be DEPENDENT upon each other for food and other needs. The group of plants and animals that are dependent on each other in an area is called a COMMUNITY.

IID
Within systems the INTERACTIONS of MATERIALS and ENERGY change their forms and properties. A group of interacting objects is called a SYSTEM.

IIIA
LIVING THINGS are affected by and AFFECT the ENVIRONMENT.

IIIC
ENERGY may exist WITHIN a MATERIAL or in the POSITION or MOTION of OBJECTS.

IIIB
ENVIRONMENTAL CONDITIONS in an area DETERMINE the types and sizes of POPULATIONS of plants and animals within a COMMUNITY and affect the way the population interacts.

IIID
MATERIAL and ENERGY can be TRANSFERRED several times within a complex SYSTEM through a series of INTERACTIONS.

IIIE
Energy and material can be transferred in an ECOSYSTEM.

LEVEL I (Ages 4 to 7)

Be sure that program activities involve: plants and animals that are familiar to students, easily maintained, and readily accessible; and objects and events, including interactions, that are familiar to students and readily accessible.

LEVEL I I (Ages 7 to 9)

Be sure that program activities involve: flowering plants and animals familiar to students, simple communities that are easily maintained and readily accessible; and properties and forms of materials and energy that can be experienced directly and systems that are familiar to students.

LEVEL III (Ages 9 to 11)

Be sure that program activities involve: green plant populations, animal populations and environmental conditions that illustrate interactions; conditions and/or complex systems that illustrate material and energy interactions, and interactions in ecosystems. All of these activities should be familiar to students and be readily accessible.

quence of the content (for New York State it is implied only in terms of three age-related levels: I, II, and III) is usually established by you.

You'll notice that even in New York, where an educational governing body, the Board of Regents exercises considerable control over what is taught in the state's schools, the details of what topics are taught in each grade (i.e., the sequence) is left up to the local schools and districts. It might be worthwhile examining the rest of the New York Syllabus' science content scope and sequence. Also, beyond all of these suggestions for science content coverage, the New York Elementary Science Syllabus offers guidance to improve the other three major areas of the science program—attitudes, skills, and problem solving. You can get more information about obtaining a copy of the New York State Elementary Science Syllabus by writing the New York State Education Department (at the address listed at the end of this chapter). Or, better yet, write to your own state's Education Department and request information on your state elementary science syllabus or guidelines.

INTEGRATING SCIENCE WITH OTHER SUBJECTS

We haven't given much time to discussing how to incorporate science into other content areas and vice versa. It actually isn't difficult if you think about it a little in advance. Even though hands-on exploration is important, there are times when a little book work will not only allow the students to collect the information they need but also improve their reading and research skills. One teacher we know does something called DEAR time with students—Drop Everything and Read! Using textbooks, encyclopedias, science trade books, magazine articles, and newspaper clippings gives students in-depth information about different topics of interest. There almost always seem to be strikingly beautiful color photographs in children's science readings as well. Some are listed at the end of this chapter.

Reading and Language Arts needs to be a focus in a science program because, although many children are often good readers, they still need direct instruction in several areas such as vocabulary, critical and creative reading, story telling, and research skills. Very often the technical vocabulary of science can be a stumbling block to comprehending content material. Some teachers we know do a "science word of the day" to help students understand and use the words of science. Crossword puzzles and word hunts provide vocabulary development and many opportunities to make use of new words.

Since a major component of science is the reporting of findings, it is a natural for integration with the writing curriculum. Daily journals about the hatching of frog eggs and their development into tadpoles and frogs encourages repeated practice in clear descriptive writing. Persuasive essays greatly benefit from the student's inclusion of science facts. Thorough description of an experimental plan encourages logical organization of a piece of writing. All these activities fit in well with the recent curriculum trend toward Whole Language.

Probably the most obvious subject for integration with science is mathematics. In collecting and analyzing data, there is a continuous need for things like graphing and calculating averages and totals. Not only do students get practice performing these math skills, they also see situations where they are useful. Perhaps that is the best reason for attempting to integrate different curricula—students see where their schooling, in all its various components, is important and fits together to make them better and more capable people. They can solve problems by using all the tools from school: reading, writing, mathematics—and science!

LOOKING BACK

This might be a good time for you to write down some of the things you feel will be an integral part of your own science program. Locate your state, district, or school plan for teaching science. Review this formal guideline. Decide how your own philosophies fit into the overall plan. Will you be able to teach your students the content, instill in them positive science attitudes, and give them opportunities to learn and practice important science-related skills? Will your students solve problems? Will what you teach fit in easily with other subject areas and with what the students have learned and will be learning in the future? A tall order, now's the time to start planning!

SELF-TEST

- Toward which of the science program philosophies do you lean for science teaching style?

- Discuss S-APA, SCIS, and ESS in relation to the programs of the 90's.

- What is the status of your home state's elementary science syllabus or guidelines?

- What does it mean to integrate science teaching with other disciplines?

- Could you outline a unit that would integrate science, reading, and langauage arts?

REFERENCES FROM RESEARCH

Linn, M. (1980). Free choice experiments: how do they help students learn? *Science Education*, 64(2), 237–248.

Padilla, M., Okey, J. and Dillashaw, F. (1983). The relationship between science process skills and formal thinking abilities. *Journal of Research in Science Teaching*, 20(3), 239–246.

Shymansky, J. A., Kyle, W. C., Jr. and Alport, J. M. (1983). The effects of new science curricula on student performance. *Journal of Research in Science Teaching*, 20(5), 387–404.

Thiel, R. and George, D. (1976). Some factors affecting the use of the science process skill of prediction by elementary school children. *Journal of Research in Science Teaching*, 62, 155–166.

PRACTICAL RESOURCES

Bybee, R., et al, (1984). *Activities for teaching about science and society.* Columbus, Ohio: Merrill.

"Hands On!," a newsletter for Technical Education Research Centers (TERC), 1696 Massachusetts Avenue, Cambridge, MA 02138.

K-8 Science Helper CD-ROM. This compact disc contains nearly 1,000 lesson plans culled from past National Science Foundation education grants like SAPA, COPES, SCIS, ESSP, USMES, MINNIMAST, and ESS. It is set up as a data base that can be searched by topic, grade level, process skill, and so on. It is available from PC-SIG, 1030 D East Duane Avenue, Sunnyvale, CA 94086, (408) 730-9291.

Lowery, L. (1985). *The everyday science sourcebook: ideas for teaching in the elementary and middle school.* Palo Alto, Calif: Dayle Seymour.

Mager, R. (1962). *Preparing instructional objectives.* Palo Alto, Calif: Fearon Publishers.

National Science Teachers Association, *Elementary Science Packets,* 1742 Connecticut Avenue, NW, Washington, DC 20009

National Science Teachers Association, *Safety in the Elementary science classroom,* 1742 Connecticut Avenue, NW, Washington, DC 20009

National Science Resources Center, *Science for children: resources for teachers,* National Academy Press, 2101 Constitution Avenue, NW, Washington, DC 20418.

Schmidt, V. and Rockcastle, V. (1982). *Teaching science with everyday things.* New York: McGraw Hill.

U.S. Department of Health, Education and Welfare. *Sources of free and low-cost materials,* Superintendent of Documents, Government Printing Office, Washington, DC 20402.

SCIS, SCIS II, SCIS III, and ESS materials are available from Delta Education, Inc., PO Box M, Nashua, NH 03061. SAPA II is distributed by Ginn and Company, 191 Spring Street, Lexington, MA 02173.

You might want to find out more about the New York State Regent's science syllabus. Contact them at

New York State Education Department
Division of Program Development
Albany, NY 12234
(518) 473-1265

Following are addresses of publishers of the new elementary science programs:

AIMS Education Foundation
PO Box 7766
Fresno, CA 93747
(209) 291-1766

BSCS
1115 N. Cascade Ave.
Colorado Springs, CO 80903

FOSS
Center for Multisensory Learning
Lawrence Hall of Science
University of California
Berkeley, CA 94720

GEMS, Lawrence Hall of Science
University of California
Berkeley, CA 94720
(415) 642-7771

The Science Mini-Museum Construction Kits
Silver, Burdett & Ginn Publishers
250 James St. CN 1918
Morristown, NJ 07960
(201) 285-8100

INSIGHTS
Education Development Center
55 Chapel Street
Newton, MA 02160

Life Lab Science Program
1156 High Street,
Santa Cruz, CA 95064

Super Science, Scholastic, Inc.
2931 East McCarty Street
PO Box 3710, Department 6001
Jefferson City, MO 65102-9957

Technical Education Resource Center
1696 Massachusetts Avenue
Cambridge, MA 02138

Following are equipment suppliers (there are many more, check with your colleagues, especially for local sources):

Carolina Biological Supply
2700 York Road
Burlington, NC 27215
(800) 334-5551

Central Scientific
1122 Melrose Avenue
Chicago, IL 60131
(312) 451-0150

Edmund Scientific
E910 Edscorp Building
Barrington, NJ 08007
(609) 573-6250

Fisher Scientific
4901 W. Lemoyne Street
Chicago, IL 60651
(800) 621-4769

Optical Data Corporation
30 Technology Drive
Warren, NJ 07059
(800) 524-2481

Sargent-Welch
7350 N. Linder Avenue
Skokie, IL 60077
(312) 677-0600

Science Kit/Boreal Labs
777 E. Park Drive
Tonawanda, NY 14150
(716) 874-6020

Ward's Natural Science Establishment
3000 Ridge Road E.
Rochester, NY 14622
(716) 467-8400

Voyage of the Mimi
Sunburst Communications
39 Washington Avenue
Pleasantville, NY 10570-2898
(800) 431-1934

5 Teaching Children about Themselves, Plants, and Animals

LOOKING AHEAD

In this and the following chapters we will be focusing, not so much on content as you might expect (or hope) but instead on places where children have trouble understanding science, some ideas for different approaches to subject areas, and some of the management problems of keeping living things in the classroom. We can't possibly cover all the science content children need to learn and still deal with the important pedagogical issues. Many soon-to-be teachers are bothered by this approach, perhaps fearing their own lack of science knowledge. But, as we've discussed in earlier chapters, it isn't your job to have all the answers. Of course, your understanding of a content area can make it easier to organize and present material and add to activities, but you must also try to place some of the burden for collecting and delivering information on your students. Give them the tasks of a scientist rather than "spilling the beans" about the content and taking away most of the fun of discovery (and ownership).

CAN YOU?

- Discuss why teaching children about themselves is different from teaching them about other things?

- Discuss some of the advantages and disadvantages of growing plants or keeping animals in the classroom?

- Suggest some of the naive ideas that children might have about plants and animals?

- Discuss strategies for correcting some of these plant and animal misconceptions?

BEING RECEPTIVE TO STUDENT QUESTIONS

We've talked about this before—a lot! It can sometimes be difficult. Juggling the immediate interests of your students with the demands of the science program or syllabus requires flexibility. Make sure you know what topics you want to cover by the end of the year. If an opportunity arises to start a unit early, perhaps you should go ahead and pursue it. If a student question or some current event preempts your plans, you will need to think (on your feet) about whether it is worth the time and effort it will take to do justice to the topic. Consider the following situation. What does it reveal about the preparation and flexibility of the teacher?

Julie: Ms. Johnson, can I ask everyone a question my sister asked at breakfast this morning?

Ms. Johnson: Sure, Julie. What is it?

Julie: My sister, Sarah, was eating a bowl of cereal and reading the stuff on the box that tells what's in it.

Ms. Johnson: You mean the nutritional information?

Julie: Yeah! It said it had iron in it. I forget how much. But it made a big deal about having vitamins and iron in it.

Andrew: Lots of cereal boxes say that!

Julie: I know. Its on all the commercials! Anyway, Sarah wanted to know how we can eat iron. Is it different than the kind of iron like our desks have in them?

Ms. Johnson: That's a good question! Does anyone know the answer? [Wait-time of 10 to 15 seconds] Well, how do we find out? How do you tell if something is iron or not? Is there any test or measurement you can think of that helps us decide if there is iron in something?

Wait-Time

Researchers have discovered that the amount of time teachers wait for student responses to their questions has an effect on the kinds of thinking the students do. These wait-time studies, as they are called, show that longer wait-times encourage higher level thinking. Amazingly, for typical teachers the average time between asking a question and either selecting a student or saying something else was about one second—hardly enough wait-time to think up a good answer! Although it's hard, wait a while (at least 4 to 5 seconds) after you ask a question. Let your students know that a well thought-out answer is worth the wait.

Erin: Oh, oh, I know! It sticks to a magnet! Right?

Andrew: Don't be stupid! Cereal doesn't stick to a magnet!

Ms. Johnson: Andrew! We need to show respect for others' ideas! How do you know it doesn't stick? Have you ever tried it?

Andrew: Sorry, Erin. I never really tried to get cereal to stick to a magnet, but I bet it doesn't.

Ms. Johnson: Well, it sounds to me like we have an experiment in the making! What's our plan?

Julie: I can bring in the box to show everybody what it says. Then we can stick a magnet into a bowl of the cereal and see if it sticks.

Andrew: I already know what's going to happen—nothing!

Ms. Johnson: Before we jump to any conclusions, we need to make a test. Iron does stick to magnets. And the cereal is supposed to contain iron. If the iron is the same kind as is in your desks it should stick to the magnet. Can anybody think of any reason why it wouldn't work?

James: Maybe there is only a tiny, little bit of iron in the cereal. The pull of the magnet wouldn't be big enough to pick up the rest of the cereal too.

Ms. Johnson: Good point! What do we do about it?

Erin: We can smash up the cereal into little pieces. Maybe the magnet would pick them up then.

Ms. Johnson: OK. Why don't we try it. Julie, you bring in your cereal and I'll bring the magnet. I remember reading about an experiment like this. I'll do a little research tonight, too.

The next day

Julie: Ms. Johnson, here's the box of cereal we talked about yesterday.

Ms. Johnson: Thanks, Julie. OK, here's a bunch of paper cups. Each workgroup take one and fill it about a third of the way up with cereal. Then put in just a little water and use one of these special magnets to mash it up.

James: Yuck!

Ms. Johnson: I know, it doesn't look too good with water on it, does it? Be careful not to spill any. Once it's mashed well, take a close look at your magnets. What do you observe?

Julie: I don't see anything. Hmm. Wait a minute. Look at all the little black dots. They weren't there before. Is that the iron?

Ms. Johnson: What do you think?

Julie: Well, it sticks to our magnet. See, you can slide it around on it. I bet that's it.

Erin: You mean we actually eat that stuff? Won't it hurt us?

Ms. Johnson: It really is iron, but it is in very, very small pieces which our stomachs can dissolve.

Andrew: Yum! I'm gonna take a bite out of my desk!

Ms. Johnson: Andrew!

Sometimes science is found in very unexpected places. What made this particular classroom session work was the experience and knowledge of Ms. Johnson. She had remembered reading in a teacher's magazine about mashing up iron-fortified cereal and pulling out the mineral with some kind of a special magnet. She looked up the article in her own computer data base of teaching ideas and found a reference to the magazine. She found the article, much as she had remembered it. It even explained that the special magnets were white Teflon-coated stirring bars, used by chemists and biologists to automatically mix solutions while they are heating. (A special hot plate provides heat and makes the stirring bar spin around at the bottom of a flask or beaker.) These magnets are strong and, very important here, covered with white Teflon. The iron particles in the cereal are so small that, even though they will stick to a conventional bar magnet, they probably won't be seen. But against the white coating of the stirring bars they show up quite well. Ms. Johnson has a friend who teaches at the local college and who was more than willing to give her a couple of stirring bars, as long as she reported the results of the students' experiment; she didn't quite believe it herself!

There were several important lessons the children learned from Ms. Johnson's impromptu science experiment. Don't jump to conclusions about an experiment. Nature has the answer, we just have to set things up so we can find out what it is. Ms. Johnson works hard at knowing things. She even has magazines that teach her interesting stuff. She also knows how to find something she read earlier. A teacher's background knowledge of a specific science topic is very important in making the lesson successful. You can be sure that more than a few parents were amazed at the nutritional information their children shared with them at the supper table that night!

Another important thing to note about Ms. Johnson's handling of the lesson is that she probably remembered that she wanted to cover nutrition at some point during the school year. Her original plans called for discussing it right after talking about digestion. She decided that capitalizing on the students' interest would result in better learning. She also considered the fact that this lesson did not require much prerequisite knowledge that might have been missed if this particular aspect of nutrition were taught earlier and somewhat out of context. The general purpose of providing a carefully designed curriculum is to provide that context and ensure coverage of important content in an organized fashion. It serves as a general guide and, as you have just seen, can be somewhat flexible. Let's look at some of the other life science topics that are usually taught in elementary classrooms.

THE HUMAN BODY

External Features

It can be really fun to teach children about their bodies. They usually are very interested in how they work. But even though things like bones, joints, and some blood vessels can be detected from outside the body, many children simply don't believe that their insides are really like the drawings. It might help to have them talk about when they or someone in their family had broken bones, a sprained ankle ligament, or perhaps an operation. Let them feel their own joints and muscles working as they move their arms and legs. Show them Harvey's demonstration of blood circulation using the veins in the forearm. (If you don't know what that is, here's a chance for you to look it up and start your own data base of materials for teaching.) Demonstrate reflexes for them, but watch out for a few trying too hard to see if their friends have reflexes! The key is to get them to realize that their bodies really do work the way it says in books. This is a situation where you can't have as many hands-on experiments as you would like. It is impossible to have everyone directly examine the heart to see if it really has four chambers. But you can have them measure their pulse rate before and after exercise. Perform as many of these simple experiments as you can. Supplement them with drawings and photographs of the internal organs and systems. Check the practical references at the end of this chapter for more ideas.

Organization of the Body

A well-accepted way of talking about the human body is by organizing the different parts into systems that accomplish specific tasks. For example, the digestive system works to bring food into the body and convert it into usable fuel. The circulatory system takes that fuel and moves it to where it is needed, along with oxygen to burn it. It then takes the waste products to where they can be eliminated, either through excretion or exhaling. In other words, the body is like a complex machine—all the parts work together. You might want to have students make up a little play where each person is a different body part. They can pass index cards representing food, oxygen, and carbon dioxide around to each other. As strange as that seems, it helps them remember what each part does because they can relate to what each classmate was doing. "Oh, yeah, Sally was the heart and Jill was blood. Sally sent Jill over to Joey. He was a lung. He took Jill's carbon dioxide card and gave her an oxygen card. Then Jill went back to Sally and then brought the oxygen card out to the rest of us."

As we've mentioned before, the secret to teaching children science is to get them involved. Rather than tell them about different kinds of taste buds, let them explore their own tongues with vinegar, sugar water, lemon juice, and salt water on cotton-tipped swabs— and then map their tongues according to taste! When they are learning about the circulatory system, let them hook up a microcomputer to graph their pulse rate as they change their activity levels. Any time the children are doing something (some might call it playing) they are learning something. It is your job to make sure that what they are learning is the science content and attitudes dictated by your science program or syllabus.

Foods and Nutrition

Nutrition is a subject that children seem to enjoy a lot. Have them do some library research about the four food groups. If you can find it, bring in information about the suggested replacement for the four food categories called the "food pyramid," which stresses limiting fats in the diet. Have the children compare the "old" four food groups to the "new" food pyramid. Children like looking at the meals they eat and making sure they contain all the essentials. You might want to bring in copies of the school cafeteria's menu for them to analyze. You can be almost certain that the meals are well balanced. (If you can, invite the person who plans the school menu for a discussion of how it is done; maybe even invite in a professional nutritionist.) Many of the fast food restaurants now provide nutritional information leaflets to those who ask for them. If your cafeteria staff is open to the idea, you might even have your children "design" a special meal that includes their favorites from each food group. They might also have to learn a little bit about economics and food prices, as well as preparation time. If this can't be done at school for practical reasons, encourage them to help their parents come up with interesting, but healthy, meals. Perhaps they could even put together a class recipe book of healthy foods.

More on the Body

Rather than simply listing typical objectives for what is often taught at the elementary level about the human body, let's look at a set of questions that you might use to generate student interest.

At the primary level, a series of questions about our senses can also incorporate some beginning ideas about scientific (that is, systematic) observation. Consider presenting something to them like a lemon or an orange and asking, "What can we learn by looking carefully at (or listening to, or smelling, or touching, or tasting) this?" Not only does this get them to be close observers, but you might also begin to see them classifying objects by their appearance or by some other observable characteristic—another important science process skill. A touch box, nothing more than a shoe box with a hand-sized hole in it, can help students concentrate on that particular sense. Closing eyes and pinching noses closed can help when studying taste. This might also be an excellent time to raise student awareness of people with limited sensory capabilities.

A fun game to play, which stresses observation and classification and also acts to bridge into another topic on the human body is to have children bring in photographs taken when they were younger. By having other students match the earlier pictures to present appearance, they often must look very carefully. This also emphasizes some of the changes they and their friends have been going through. The early grades offer plenty of opportunities to talk about growing bodies. You probably don't have to plan a specific time to discuss teeth getting loose and coming out—you can be sure it will be brought up by many of your students when it happens to them!

The different systems of the body can be brought into a classroom discussion by asking questions like, "Now that we are back from the cafeteria, what is going to happen to your lunch?" "Why do you have to breathe?" "Why is it so important for a cut to stop bleeding? What does blood do, anyway?" "Do you have any muscles besides those in your arms?" (This is directed toward a common misconception. Many students think their biceps are their only muscles—although talkative children may have been told by their parents that they have big cheek muscles!) Once you establish that there are muscles all over the body, you can ask children how muscles can all work together to make the body run or walk. You might try having the children make a cardboard leg with knee and ankle joints. You can simulate muscles by pairs of strings that the children pull on to make the "leg" move realistically. They quickly recognize the importance of coordinating muscles. This is the time to begin a discussion of the brain and nervous system.

It is probably never too early to begin teaching children about ways to keep their bodies healthy. You can promote this by classroom rules such as, "Walk with a scissors." "Wash your hands before eating, after going to the bathroom, and after working with the classroom plants and animals." "Cover your mouth when you cough or sneeze." Encourage your students to understand the reasons for these rules—not because you want them to question your authority, but because in understanding the purpose of the rules, they'll learn lots of science. Explore! Experience!

In the upper elementary grades you can study the body in more detail. Rather than just discussing what the different senses are, students can now begin to understand how they work. Large diagrams of the inside of the eye and ear help them conceptualize things they cannot see. You might want to get some lenses and ask students to use them to make a miniature eye. Ask them why people wear glasses. When talking about hearing, discuss hearing aids and maybe have the school nurse give them a hearing test (which will normally be done from time to time, anyway). Talk about the importance of avoiding loud sounds. Tell them that listening to very loud music now might mean they won't be able to hear it as well (or enjoy it as much) when they get older. The varying sensitivity of the skin to touch is easy to explore. Let the children bend paper clips into a U shape. They can adjust the separation of the two tips and use that to *gently* touch different parts of their partner's skin. With the partner's eyes closed, have them touch the palm and back of the hand, forearm, shin, and fingertips. They can adjust the tips until the partner is able to tell if one or two tips are touching them. Ask the children why they think the different parts of the body vary so much in their touch sensitivity. (Actually, the skin that covers our bodies is very sensitive to touch. But how sensitive different parts of the body is, varies. Body places with many nerve endings are very sensitive— such as the fingertips, which will sense both tips of the paper clip. A less sensitive area, such as the back of your hand, may not be able to distinguish between one or two paper-clip points.)

The different parts of the heart and how they function are complex ideas, but learnable. You might quickly show the children a picture or diagram of the four chambers and discuss what they do, and then ask the students to think up ways to help them remember the different parts and their functions. You might want to go to the local butcher shop and get a beef heart to show your students. They might suggest a game where they put a large masking tape model of the body on the floor and walk back and forth through the heart, to the lungs, back to the heart, and out to the rest of the body. Encouraging this metacognitive activity helps children learn the science content, and also helps them learn how to learn!

The purpose and operation of the circulatory system does not seem to be too difficult for children to understand. They don't appear to have many misconceptions about how it operates. After talking about the different components of the system, you might ask students how many times a person's heart beats in a day, week, or even an entire lifetime. This not only gives them a chance to practice math, it also impresses them with the workings of the body.

Moving from a discussion of the circulatory system to the skeletal system can often be done by discussing that red blood cells are made in bone marrow. Most students do not realize that bones have vessels that are so important to the circulatory system. Often they think of bones as dry, dead "sticks." After talking about the nature of living bones, ask them why it is so common to think of bones as dry and without blood supply. You also might want to ask what their bodies would be like if they didn't have any bones. (If you can, find a short video of a jellyfish as it moves through the water.) Try the local butcher again; this time, ask for a long bone, and have him or her cut it lengthwise to expose that important part called the bone marrow.

When discussing the digestive system, maybe students could make a long model of the entire tract. Students often think that all digestion takes place only in the stomach. Constructing a model would be a way of showing them that the stomach has an important role, but there are other things going on as well. You could start with a pair of nutcrackers to represent the teeth. Put a piece of clay into a small plastic bag (mouth or oral cavity). The clay will be the food to be digested. The bag keeps the clay together, helps it slide down the esophagus, and makes cleanup easier. A long sock (with the toes cut out) for the esophagus lets the students push the food along by squeezing just behind it with their hands (an action called *peristalsis*), a stomach made of a larger plastic bag allows students to knead the food into smaller pieces (stomach muscle action). The small and large intestines can also be long socks or perhaps nylons to represent the places where nutrients and water are removed from the food (a very important part of digestion). Finally, another small bag at the end can represent the rectum where the undigestible parts of the food are stored for later elimination. As the children do more research work and learn more about the real digestive tract, they might add things like salivary glands, bile duct, and a pancreas to their model.

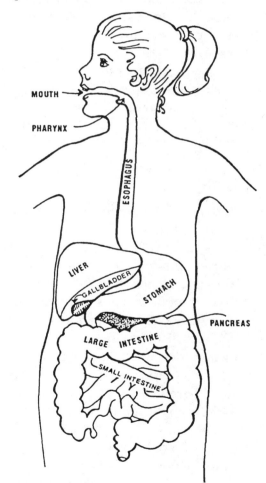

Diagram of the Digestive System

PLANTS

Common Misconceptions

Children, even though they are around plants all their lives (or perhaps *because* they are around plants so much) have many mistaken ideas about them. You can bring these problems out by asking questions like, "Are there any plants that don't grow in a garden?" "Are trees (or seeds or weeds) plants?" "Can plants ever get too much water (or food or sun)?" Sometimes children have a hard time realizing that plants are alive. They tend to relate movement to life. The sun, wind, and clouds are alive since they move. Trees are not because they don't. (Besides, trees are made of wood like a door, which obviously isn't alive!) Fires are also alive because they move, "eat" wood, and need air. As is typical of most misconceptions, there are some correct ideas in there somewhere, but often they are misapplied or incomplete. You need to diagnose your students' naive ideas, get them to closely examine these ideas, and help them change their ideas to more appropriate ones by doing activities and solving problems that deal with the topics related to their naive ideas.

Characteristics of Plants

Younger students can be encouraged to talk about seeds that blow around, stick to clothes, get discarded from fruit, or pass through a digestive tract. Primary school children will enjoy making their own "pocket garden" from a moist piece of paper towel between two glass microscope slides held together with rubber bands. Small seeds (like carrot or radish seeds) placed on the towel (keep it moist) will germinate within a day or two. Since light isn't needed for germination (conflicting with a common misconception), children can take their gardens with them to show their friends and family.

Leaves, roots, stems, and flowers are usually sufficiently distinct so that even young scientists can identify them. You may also want to show an exception, like the poinsettia. (The flower is really just the small yellowish part in the center of the bright red leaves.) A good activity for older children is to dissect flowers that you have obtained from the florist (tulips and gladiolas work well). Identification of sepals, petals, stigma, style, and ovary (pistil, or female portion of the flower) and anther and filament (stamen, or male portion of the flower) can lead to interesting discussions of plant reproduction. Ask the children to identify the stem of a tree (transporter and supporter) and compare it to the roots (anchor and absorber). All of these plant parts are remarkable structures.

Most children will readily note that plants are green. They can usually collect lots of different kinds of leaves for wall displays. Be sure also to let students examine some mushrooms or another nonproducing plant. Around Flag Day, split the stems of several white carnations into thirds. Place one stem section into a small vial of red-colored water, another into blue water, and the last into clear water. With any luck you will soon have a very patriotic science demonstration (due to a process called capillary action)!

Older children can begin to look at plant cells and their specialized parts. By fifth or sixth grade, students can more thoroughly understand photosynthesis and grasp the central role of food-producing plants in the ecosystem. All ages can benefit from carefully examining plant tissue with a magnifying lens. Onion skin, when observed very closely, reveals a clear cell structure. On another note, although most plants display limited motion, a few can move fairly rapidly. A sundew or venus fly trap can lead to very interesting discussions. Have students dissect pieces of celery. (Be sure to tell them the roots have already been cut off.) Have them place some celery into a glass of colored water. After about an hour the tubes that carry water up to the leaves should be colored. Ask your students to compare these tubules to blood vessels. This is a nice follow-up to the red, white, and blue carnation science demonstration.

Variation in Plants

Ask students to describe some of the differences between plants. What do they think causes plants to vary so much? How do people use plants? Obviously, many food products come from plants. Also point out some of the wooden and paper products in the room. Most students don't think of these things as originally coming from plants. If you can, bring in a cotton boll and some cotton cloth.

Young children can categorize (classify) actual plants that you have brought into the classroom or photographs that they have snipped from magazines. Ask them to form their own categories. They are usually pretty good at this. You will be surprised at all the different ways they come up with to differentiate one plant from another. Older students might be able to put together their own plant guidebook to help them in identifying plants. A leaf collection can often be a highly motivating exercise. Having the children compare their leaf classification schemes to those found in the library's guidebooks can be very enlightening.

Requirements for Life

Ask students if plants could live on just water. (Set up an experiment and try it!) Is it more important to water the leaves of the plant (a common belief) or the soil the plant's roots are in? Have them do experiments to see if it is possible to overwater plants. Many students think food comes into the plant from the soil. (Actually, plants can absorb water-soluble minerals through their roots, but the real "building blocks" come from water and air.) Ask students to consider plants that grow for years in a small pot with very little soil. (If they don't recognize the problem, mention that the food in the soil would run out eventually.) It can be very difficult for children to understand that plants make their own food from sunlight, water, and air. This is obviously quite different from the way their bodies work. Have them try to grow some plants in the dark. Older students can learn about the transportation of water through a plant by enclosing the stem and leaves of a small plant in a plastic bag that is closely tied to the stem. Ask them where the water droplets come from that form on the inside of the bag.

Plant Reproduction

Planting seeds and watching them grow is often the first science experiment for many primary school children. Seed growth takes time (although beans normally sprout in less than a week), but it is usually highly rewarding. There are many variables that the children can control. The amount of sunlight, depth of planting, and the amount of water can all be easily varied to discover the effect on germination and the young plants. Even though the outer parts of seeds can be quite different, the inner components are remarkably similar. Have your students take apart peanuts, pine cone seeds, seeds from grapefruit or apples, maple keys, acorns, beans, corn, peas, and whatever other seeds they can find. (Make sure they wash their hands after working with any seeds or plants.)

A careful examination of seeds will reveal the little plant inside (embryo) and the food for it (cotyledons, or stored food). Have the students grow some bean seeds with none, one, and both halves of the food portion removed. An attempt to germinate seeds in the dark will show that they really do contain food. (Before this is done, students must understand that sunlight provides energy to make the food that the mature plant produces from air and water.)

Older children can begin to appreciate the structure and purpose of flowers on plants. It also is nice to explore the different ways pollen can travel from one plant to another. Seed transport is very interesting and is something children can relate to, since they probably have played with dandelion seeds and maple keys, and have brought thistle seeds home when the seeds stuck to their clothes. Be sure to show children some flowering trees and grasses — not all flowers are bright and colorful. Try the following science teaching activity with your second graders.

SCIENCE ACTIVITY TO TRY

SEED DISPERSAL

The events that make up the story of seed dispersal are fascinating. Dispersal is vital to the life of a seed and its subsequent development into a mature plant. Many seeds are equipped with marvelous devices that allow them to travel far from their origin. The maple seed has helicopter-like appendages that cause it to "fly" to its resting place when snatched by a sudden gust of wind. The burdock has tiny hooks that catch onto unwary travelers, finally to be released at a planting site. The wild geranium shoots seeds away from the parent plant by means of a slingshot mechanism. Other seeds are protected by a thick, fleshy portion, the fruit, often eaten by birds and animals and deposited later in a natural fertilizer. Seeds have countless methods by which to travel. There are numerous possibilities for activities related to the story of seed dispersal.

Title: Seed Dispersal

Skills: Observing, inferring, classifying

Content: Seed dispersal, seeds, plants, germination

Materials: Magnifying glasses, construction paper, Ziploc bags

Procedure: Either take the children outside to gather seeds (in the fall) in their Ziploc bags or you bring in a variety of wild seeds. Simple magnifying glasses will help children locate the different appendages, hooks, flaps, and so on, that allow seeds to travel. A chart could be constructed, categorizing each seed as to its adaptations for dispersal. Discussions should include the importance of seed dispersal to the life of the seed. Finally, provide the necessary materials for the children to germinate and plant some of the wild seeds, thus testing their various inferences. An open container, tap water, and paper toweling positioned so that seeds can "breathe" are all the equipment you need.

A first project might be the construction of individual seed collages (art too!). The children should be challenged to devise plans before assembling their collages. Each child should be able to explain in a written description the meaning of his or her creation to the rest of the class. Construction of the seed collages thus becomes a thought-provoking activity requiring certain strategies and advance planning. An interesting "outdoor art" display case or bulletin board could be made using the completed projects.

Closure: Write down or draw two special "adaptations" that seeds have that allow them to move to a favorable place to begin growth.

Plants that reproduce without producing seeds can make an interesting study. If there is a forest nearby, it should be fairly easy to collect some moss and ferns. Try growing some bread mold and letting the students examine it with a magnifying glass. These nonseed-producing kinds of plants produce microscopic, round bodies called spores to reproduce more of their own kind.

Plant Adaptations

Many of the variations between types of plants are the result of the plant species adjusting to the environment around them. Most students (and adults, for that matter) have no idea that pine needles are actually leaves. Have your students look up where different kinds of pine trees grow. They will find that most are in colder climates. Since the summer season is fairly short, the needles must stay on the tree all year in order to make enough food for the plant to survive. But the needles must have a small surface area so that the trees don't dehydrate in the cold winds. The needles actually help conserve water for these trees. In warmer climates, deciduous trees lose their leaves during the colder parts of the year. Since they don't have to "worry" about dehydration during the colder months, leaves that form during the warmer season usually have larger surface areas and so are better at absorbing sunlight.

Besides leaves, the stems, roots, and flowers of plants have adapted themselves to the conditions they grow in. Have students compare dandelion roots to those of clover. Ask "Why are the root systems different?" Different flowers have arisen to make the most of the pollen transport system available (either weather related or carried by animals). We've already discussed some of the differences in seeds. Ask students why trees, which grow in crowded forests, have such tall, strong stems. They probably never even thought of it before. If you can, bring in a picture of a tulip (poplar) tree, which, when growing in a forest, has a characteristically tall, straight trunk.

ANIMALS

Common Misconceptions

Children tend to give human attributes to animals, perhaps from watching cartoons where the animal characters can walk, talk, and think. For example, your students may believe that all animal parents care for their young as humans do. They may think of certain animals as having particular, human-like personalities (a St. Bernard is good, a wolf is bad). Also, many students mistakenly believe that all animal senses are like their own. When you think about it, the most direct way to relate to a dog's sense of smell, for example, is by imagining it to be just like yours. Looked at positively, these ideas provide a platform or foundation on which to build correct concepts if the teacher is aware of youngsters' misconceptions comparing human and animal senses. You can see how children's knowledge of their own senses helps them more easily understand animal senses by comparing student difficulty with learning about a particular animal's sight or hearing and when they try to grasp the purpose of a fish's lateral line or a bird's magnetic sense for navigation, things that have no human equivalent. It is clear that initial ideas based on one's experience have a major impact on learning later on. It is up to you, the teacher, to make the best of the situation—starting with an awareness that the children's conceptions are different than yours.

A fairly common belief held by elementary school students is that animals have four legs and fur. This means that they don't consider insects, worms, or birds to be animals. In general, children's "animals" are found on land, which excludes fish, whales, snails, and so on. You probably are already aware that people of all ages often think that whales and dolphins are fish. What has happened is that people categorize animals based on inappropriate characteristics. Probably the best approach here is to explicitly state the ways scientists have grouped animals into such classes as mammal, amphibian, and so on. Have a classification lab activity: Put out examples of animals that have to be put into the appropriate group. (It is always fun to have children learn these classification schemes and then let them figure out what to do with some of the more unusual creatures like the duck-billed platypus!) One of the most difficult misconceptions to overcome is that humans are not animals. The best route here is probably to define animals in general and discuss the things they have in common. It then is not too hard for children to imagine how humans fit in as a mammal-animal.

Characteristics of Animals

An easy transition into the study of the animal kingdom is by comparing the sensory capability of various animals to that of humans and looking at why they might be different. You can ask your students if they know of any animals that can hear better than humans (such as dogs) or that can see better at night (such as cats). Not only does this motivate children to learn, it also directly addresses their misconceptions. They learn ways that animals are alike (most have similar senses) and ways that they differ (sensory sensitivity varies greatly). They also find out about different needs of animals and how those needs affect physical characteristics.

Some teachers like to approach this subject from the cellular level. For the later elementary grades this might be appropriate, but younger students may find the ideas too abstract. If you decide to use this approach, be sure to supplement microscope labs with colorful drawings. This way, you can be sure everyone knows what all the pieces look like. Note that many children have a hard time using microscopes. (Author James Thurber wrote an amusing story relating his misadventures in a biology lab, which you might want to read. Besides being humorous, it also points out some common experiences students have in lab settings.) Sources of material to examine include commercially prepared slides, student-collected pond water, or inner cheek cells smeared onto a swab.

Variety in Animals

Just as we saw when discussing children studying plants, it can be a good idea to have children categorize animals. You can begin by letting them make up their own taxonomy. Some of these might be quite useful—fish have gills, mammals have hair, birds have feathers, and so on. Later you can bring in other divisions (for example, vertebrate/invertebrate, herbivore/carnivore/omnivore). With guidance from you, they can even get specific enough to differentiate between insects and spiders. (Insects have six legs and three body sections, spiders have eight legs but only two body sections.)

To attune children to the differences between animals, try playing a "What am I?" game, starting with easier animals and ending with some that are not immediately obvious, such as the platypus, whale, shark, ostrich, or penguin. Another good approach is to have children look at different environmental conditions and think about how that might be reflected in the animals found in that region. You might focus on one particular animal feature and have children examine how that feature varies from one creature to another. For example, have them compare the teeth of grazing and hunting animals. How do human teeth compare? Since we are omnivores (we may eat both meat and vegetable matter), the children should see dental characteristics of both herbivores and carnivores. Children also seem to like to compare bird features. Beak variations can easily be linked to diet or foot shape can be related to usage or habitat preference. The advantage of this way of teaching science is that children are then able to look at an unknown animal and make educated guesses about what it eats and how it lives. You might want to prepare students for a field trip to the zoo by showing them photographs of animals and having them hypothesize animal life-styles. These could be investigated by observing the actual creatures. Read the following vignette in which Ms. Jones teaches us about science teaching and birds.

Ms. Jones has learned that Julie, one of her fifth-grade students, has a stuffed owl.

Ms. Jones: Julie, could you bring in your stuffed owl tomorrow to share and tell about?

Julie: Sure! I'll check with my mom!

The next day Julie finishes telling about how her family acquired Hooter, her stuffed barred owl, and Ms. Jones begins a lesson about owls.

Ms. Jones [with Hooter in plain view of everyone projects a drawing of a chicken on the screen]: How are the owl and the chicken alike and how are they different?

Jerome: The claws are very different. The owl's claws are huge and very sharp!

Tyrone: The eyes of the chicken are much smaller than the owl's. They're placed in the head differently, too.

Ms. Jones: Good, what else? [wait-time]

Millie: The wings on the owl are much larger.

Ms. Jones lists the student comments on the board.

Ms. Jones: An animal in the wild usually survives if it can get enough food to eat and can avoid becoming food. What do Hooter and the chicken eat?

Johnny: From the looks of Hooter's beak, he might catch little animals and eat them.

Henry: Like mice!

Mary: He probably hunts them at night, too!

Hector: I just read a great book called *The Owl Moon*. It said in the book that owls are great night hunters because they're so quick and quiet. They swoop down upon their prey without a sound.

Mrs. Jones: Does everyone know what the word *prey* means? Hector, what is prey?

Hector: It's the animal that is used for food by the predator or animal who is doing the catching and eating of the prey.

Ms. Jones: Very good. Now, what about our chicken, what does he eat?

Eli: One summer, I visited a farm and we fed the chickens chicken feed. I think it was broken up corn seeds.

Ms. Jones: Good. Now, what is it about Hooter that might help him find and capture mice?

Tyrone: Owls can hear better!

Jerome: Owl ears are sure much better for finding and catching mice than are chickens'!

Mary: Owls have front and back toes for grabbing the mice.

Malcolm: I'm not sure a real chicken has ever caught a mouse!?

Ms. Jones: Good job! Thank you. Now, take another look at Hooter. His big eyes make it easier to see at night. Having both eyes looking forward sure helps in locating objects. The front and back toes with sharp claws make it easy to grasp and hold onto things. Look at Hooter's sharp, hooked beak. It can penetrate and hold onto things and tear them apart. Look at this picture of a barred owl. Look at how its ears (hidden under the feathers) start above each eye and circle down on the front of the face to the owl's throat. Big ears on a big face make it possible for owls to hear very well. Hooter is well suited for finding and capturing mice at night.

Thank you for bringing in Hooter, Julie! OK, let's take a look at what happens after an owl eats his supper. What do you think this is? [Ms. Jones passes around an object in a bottle that looks like a fat rabbit's foot.]

SCIENCE ACTIVITY TO TRY

OWL PELLETS

Title: Owl Pellets

Skills: Observing, inferring, predicting, hypothesizing, classifying, creating models

Content: Raptors, predator, prey, owl natural history, food chains and webs

Materials: Each team of two students will have one owl pellet, two or three toothpicks, white (ditto) paper, 3 × 5 index cards, glue, paper towels, owl fact sheets

Procedure: Review science activity rules (respect partners; be careful with toothpicks and gently pick owl pellet apart; carefully clean up). What are these things? (Hold up an owl pellet) Discussion. Demonstrate how to gently separate and dissect the pellet (by teasing it apart gently). Distribute owl fact sheets to students. Read, discuss, and make predictions. Distribute remainder of owl pellet materials. Teacher circulates, helping when necessary. 3 × 5 cards can be used to glue skeleton(s) together and onto index cards. Clean up; students return materials. (3 × 5 card work might need to be continued).

Closure: What did you find in the owl pellet? What can you tell me about how owls live?

Requirements for Life

Ask children who are students in a good science program what they are doing in science and they'll most likely tell you that they are building birdfeeders, or making a terrarium, or keeping turtles or fish. Maybe they have an ant farm or they have collected cocoons or frog eggs to hatch. In other words, they are busy keeping animals in their classrooms or homes. This has many important advantages. It is immediately motivating. Children are actively involved in taking care of their animals. It affords them the opportunity to closely observe animals as they proceed through their life cycles. They can go beyond simple observations to involving the animals in humane activities. Fish can be taught to respond to a student at feeding time, for example. Hamsters soon separate their cages into dining and bathroom areas. The main thing that children learn from caring for animals is what they require to stay alive. Water and food must be given in specific amounts and at proper time intervals.

Animal Reproduction

This is an area where children have many misunderstandings of the animal world. Once they find that many animals abandon their young, usually by leaving the eggs, they think that the animal parents are cruel. It is difficult to teach them that they cannot judge animal behavior by human standards. Again, it is easy to see how life experiences shape the way students approach new knowledge. Ask the children if their parents will be taking care of them all of their lives. By getting them to realize that humans also go out on their own when they are ready helps them understand that the same thing happens with other animals. The big difference is that many animals start out ready to fend for themselves. Perhaps you can show a video of newly hatched turtles heading for the sea, or young insects that are just miniature versions of adults. This will help children recognize that reproduction and family life for many animals is different than that of humans. You can also have your students watch birds building nests or kittens being nursed, things not too remote from human experience.

By learning about animal reproduction in general, children are prepared to understand human reproduction and the changes that will be taking place in their own bodies. Although sometimes a sensitive subject, human sexuality is now taught in most elementary schools. Different districts handle sex education in a variety of ways. In some cases, it is taught as a completely separate subject. A certain time, usually toward the end of the fifth or beginning of the sixth grade, is set aside. Children have most of the details of human reproduction explained to them in a straightforward fashion, often by a teacher of the same gender. Whether your school will do this or incorporate sexuality instruction within the science program, most children have little difficulty remembering what they are taught about the subject. This is perhaps an important lesson in how motivation and interest can make a big difference in retention of information. Human reproduction is something children, even in the elementary grades, regard as very important.

INTERRELATIONSHIPS

Things Plants and Animals Have in Common

The primary grades are where children learn about living things in general. All organisms require energy input and give off waste products. Children can also start to understand how plants and animals depend on each other. Even young students can grasp the idea of plants producing food and animals consuming it. Older elementary students can more thoroughly understand the processes of photosynthesis, herbivory and carnivory. Have them look at several food chains. Ask if they know that they are "solar powered." By tracing energy from the sun, through grain to bread or through grass to cow to milk and then into them, they begin to see a larger picture of how each part of the chain depends on the other parts. Interdependence is an important concept. We'll talk more about it and other ecological issues in Chapter 9.

LOOKING BACK

We obviously could not cover every life science topic that could be taught to elementary school children. Good sources for additional guidance are some of the textbooks that are available for adoption. You should become familiar with what different publishing companies think is important—not because the companies themselves automatically know what content should be taught but because they have researched the area carefully. They have talked to teachers, teaching organizations, scientists, educational administrators, and groups of parents. Actually, that's not such a bad idea. You might want to try talking to a few people on your own!

SELF-TEST

- The local newspaper runs an article about the amazing Monarch butterfly and its grueling migration. The next day, Mary, your student brings to school a tattered, but still living Monarch butterfly in a mayonaise jar. How would you pursue this teaching opportunity?

- What's the importance of exhibiting good wait-time as a teacher?

- What is a hands-on activity that you could do to teach about the human body to second graders?

- What are some of the different mechanisms by which different seeds are dispersed into the environment in your local area? List the plant and describe the seed dispersal mechanism.

- What animal would you choose to keep in your classroom? Why?

- What "animal activities" might you promote in your classroom?

- Draw and explain a local food chain.

SCOPE AND SEQUENCE

If you remember what we discussed in Chapter 4, there is not universal agreement on when different topics should be taught. Still, beginning teachers often appreciate some kind of guidance. In that vein, consider the following suggestions. Think about how you would modify the ordering of topics to better fit your own plans.

First grade   Senses, growing, categorizing plants and animals, how people use plants and animals, needs of living things

Second grade   Parts of the body, healthy habits, parts of plants, comparing animals

Third grade   Body systems, nutrition and health, growing plants and animals, interaction of plants and animals

Fourth grade	Digestion, circulation, nervous system, plant reproduction, animal behavior, food chains, adapting to the environment
Fifth grade	Bones, muscles, respiration, growing up, animals with and without backbones, plant and animal communities
Sixth grade	Body systems, health, classifying plants and animals, cells, genetics, evolution, ecosystems

REFERENCES FROM RESEARCH

Kahle, J. (1990). *Issues in instruction: biology.* Paper prepared for the FIRST/FIPSE Conference, Washington, D.C.

Lawson, A. (1988). The acquisition of biological knowledge during childhood: cognitive conflict or tabula rasa? *Journal of Research in Science Teaching,* 25(3), 185–199.

Mintzes, J. (1989). The acquisition of biological knowledge during childhood: an alternative conception. *Journal of Research in Science Teaching,* 26(9), 823–824.

Trowbridge, J. and Mintzes, J. (1988). Alternative conceptions in animal classification: a cross-age study. *Journal of Research in Science Teaching,* 25(7), 547–571.

Wandersee, J. (1983, June). *Students' misconceptions about photosynthesis: a cross-age study.* Paper presented at the International Seminar on Misconceptions and Educational Strategies in Science and Mathematics, Ithaca, N.Y.: Cornell University, pp.441–466.

Wandersee, J., Mintzes, J. and Arnaudin, M. (1987, July). *Children's biology: a content analysis of conceptual development in the life sciences.* Paper presented at the Second International Seminar on Misconceptions and Educational Strategies in Science and Mathematics, Ithaca, N.Y.: Cornell University.

PRACTICAL RESOURCES

Allison, L. (1976). *Blood and guts.* Boston: Little, Brown.

American Biology Teacher, National Association of Biology Teachers, 1420 N Street, NW, Washington, DC 20007

Blough, G. and Schwartz, J. (1990). *Elementary school science and how to teach it.*

Chicago: Holt, Rinehart and Winston.

Dobey, D. and Pickett, S. (1980). How will I be planted: the story of seed dispersal. *The Communicator, Journal of the New York State Outdoor Education Association,* 11(1), 32–33.

Friedl, A. (1991). *Teaching science to children—An integrated approach.* New York: McGraw-Hill.

Owl Pellet Information, Pellets, Inc., 3004 Pinewood, Bellingham, WA 98225, (206) 733-3012.

Restivo, E. and Hudson, H. (1990). "Iron enriched" cereal—literally. *The Physics Teacher,* 9(28), 608.

Simpson, P. and Coulter, J. (1991). *Life science for elementary teachers.* Dubuque, Iowa: Kendall/Hunt.

Victor, E. (1989). *Science in the elementary school.* New York: Macmillan.

ZooBooks., PO Box 85384, San Diego, California 92186, (800) 992-5034.

6 Teaching Children about the Earth and the Universe

LOOKING AHEAD

Children are always interested in the world around them. The topics discussed in this chapter seem to lend themselves to highly engaging instruction. Even though your students will have misconceptions about the earth and the universe, these ideas are somehow more amenable to change. Perhaps children realize they haven't quite figured out "how all this stuff works" and so have an easier time accepting a more scientific view because the new ideas are quite simple and explain things that they have wondered about for a long time. Learning how to predict the weather and make sense of newspaper and television weather reporting gives children the ability to judge for themselves what conditions will be like for some important event in their lives. Explaining how the seasons occur answers their long-held questions and makes for an easy transition to a study of the solar system.

Besides their earth-bound interests, many children are similarly curious about the stars and planets. They really enjoy being able to recognize constellations and show their friends and parents. Although they certainly have noticed the changes in the phases of the moon, they probably have not seen the periodicity of it. It is unlikely that they have observed the changing position of the planets against the rotating sphere of stars. The nice thing about showing them "how all the pieces fit together" is that they will learn something that can be reinforced every time they are outside on a clear night.

CAN YOU?

- Relate some of the many mistaken ideas children have about the world around them and their place in it.

- Figure out where some of the aforementioned misconceptions come from?

- Use your knowledge of children's misconceptions of the universe to help your teaching? How?

- Discuss why the topic of weather is particularly appropriate for the problems approach to teaching science?

EARTH SCIENCE—A "NATURAL" TOPIC

The topics discussed in this chapter are those that surround children. Literally, it is their world! Of all the content areas in the sciences, it is probably easiest to come up with leading questions for earth science. Children always want to know more about what is happening around them. Consider the following scenario and how the teacher leads the students into it:

Mr. Holmes: OK, who knows what kind of day it's supposed to be next Thursday?

Billy: It's Activity Day!

Mr. Holmes: What does that mean? Maybe Ms. Estebán [the student teacher] hasn't heard of it yet.

Megan: That's when we get to go outside and do all kinds of neat stuff! We play games with the other grades and . . .

Billy: Yeah! It's awesome!

Mr. Holmes: Billy, it's not polite to interrupt. We need to hear what others are saying. Megan, was there something else you wanted to say?

Megan: Yeah, it is awesome!

Mr. Holmes: What I was really wondering was if any of you knew what the weather was going to be on Thursday. We might want to know if it is supposed to be nice for Activity Day. I guess my question wasn't clear enough.

Amanda: I think it's supposed to be warm and sunshiny.

Ms. Estebán: What makes you think that?

Amanda: That's what the weatherman said last night on the news.

Ms. Estebán: Well, then, what made him think that?

Amanda: He's got maps and radar and stuff.

Megan: And satellite pictures! Don't forget the satellite pictures.

Billy: What are those *barmeter* things? They're always goin' up and down.

Mr. Holmes: Do you mean a *barometer*, Billy? It's an instrument that measures air pressure. How does a weather forecaster use all these things to predict what the weather is going to be? [Silence for 10 or 15 seconds, great wait-time.] Is there any kind of limit to what they can do? How far ahead can they predict the weather?

Billy: All they do is a five-day forecast! At least that's the farthest I've seen any of them go.

Mr. Holmes: That's what I seem to remember, too. OK. How do we find out how they predict the weather? We've already decided that it somehow involves their maps, radar, satellite photos, and some special instruments. Where do we go from here?

As the class continues, the children plan their approach to finding out about weather forecasting. Eventually, they will make their own instruments, including a barometer made from straws, balloons, and cups, and a device that measures relative humidity using a milk carton and a long strand of human hair! The children want to get real satellite pictures. If the school had more money it could purchase an antenna and equipment that would actually receive weather photos from a satellite. Instead, Ms. Estebán is able to make arrangements with the local airport. The airport has generously agreed to print a few extra photos for her every morning during the next week. She will pick them up on her way to school. The children, remembering that the newspaper also has weather maps, will be clipping them out and bringing them in as well. All agree to watch the weather reports on television. Some will take notes on the predictions to compare to the newspaper version. Others will record the different factors that are reported by the weather person as having an effect on upcoming weather. These students are well on their way to some exciting lessons!

THE EARTH

There Are Many Misconceptions about the Earth and the Universe

Since your students have been living on the earth for their entire lives, they have formed quite a few opinions about it. First, a lot of children think that the earth sits on something. It certainly can't just be "floating!" (Many of your students' misconceptions have counterparts in the history books. You might want to bring in some drawings made in ancient times that show the earth supported on the back of a turtle or an elephant. Children realize that such a thing makes no sense, and hopefully, this will lead them to abandon their own misconceptions.) From observation, they believe that the earth is larger than both the moon and the sun and even though they may have heard otherwise, it is pretty obvious that the sun goes around the earth. These can be difficult conceptions to change. Others are not as problematic because children have no direct "evidence" to support their ideas, just a hunch. For example, the naive idea that the changing seasons are caused by varying distances to the sun during the year can be fairly easily displaced by the correct interpretation. The thought that the phases of the moon are caused by the earth's shadow is soon abandoned by children playing with a flashlight and an orange in a darkened room. Other common misconceptions that you can probably diagnose include the belief that the moon goes around the earth in one day, the moon makes its own light like the sun, and planets can't be seen with the naked eye. (Children get very excited when given a sky map that tells them where to look for Mars or Saturn. If they have access to good binoculars, they can even see the moons of Jupiter.)

Not surprisingly, children come up with many explanations of weather phenomena. Rain may come from holes in the clouds or from clouds sweating or from funnels in the clouds. Sometimes rain comes from melting clouds or clouds that are shaken by the wind. Because of an optical illusion, many children think that clouds move when we move, following people around from place to place. Clouds may be believed to come from the boiling of sea water by the sun. The clouds themselves are either big bags of water or made of cotton or smoke. None of these ideas is too unreasonable to a child. In fact, these ideas may seem more plausible than many of the things they hear about in school!

What is the best way to help a child work through his or her misconceptions and gain insight into certain scientific topics? Seeing it happen or *doing* it in a hands-on, experiential way may go a long way toward overcoming most misconceptions. Let's take another look at children's conceptions of clouds.

Contrary to the aforementioned misconceptions, clouds are really large groups of condensed water droplets that we can see in the sky. Winds carry clouds with them and the clouds can continue to pick up moisture (by evaporation of water) and get bigger. When clouds hit cooler air, they reduce their moisture content by releasing "heavy" drops of water back to the earth as rain. Try the following activity with your third graders.

SCIENCE ACTIVITY TO TRY

RAIN CLOUDS

Title: Rain Clouds

Skills: Observing, inferring, creating a model

Content: Weather, clouds, warm and cold fronts, evaporation, condensation

Materials: Wide-mouthed (heat-resistant) glass jar, metal pie tin, ice cubes, hot water

Procedure: Introduce a discussion of clouds by doing the following demonstration: Fill the jar with 3 to 4 centimeters of hot water.

Quickly cover the jar with the metal pie tin filled with ice cubes. Observe the formation of small clouds and "rain" droplets (on the bottom of the pie tin). More discussion about clouds.

Closure: Compare what happens in the jar to what happens outside. Ask, "What causes rain?"

The Rain Clouds activity or demonstration helps show children that as hot water heats the air, it rises, carrying moisture up to the cold pie tin. The cold pie tin causes the moisture in the air inside the jar to condense into droplets. After a short while, enough water droplets form on the bottom of the pie tin to fall down as "rain." Your students may need your help to work through this explanation and see the logic in this activity and then transfer what they have learned to real life!

What about the Weather?

Most children are fascinated to finally learn that something as simple as the tilt of the earth on its axis causes the difference between summer and winter. The brief vignette at the beginning of this chapter underscores how easy it can be to involve children in learning about weather. The teacher had a few ideas put together for some fun labs using readily available materials. The students knew they had access to lots of information in the daily news reports. Together they mapped out a plan for finding out more about weather forecasting, something of great interest to the students.

Combining what children have learned about the earth and its climates makes an easy introduction to the topics of geography and social studies. If possible, bring many different areas of study together. Remember that the division of content into separate subject areas is completely contrived. In the real world, most things are connected to everything else. Help children see that. They have a hard enough time transferring learning from one setting to another. Don't make it more difficult for them by setting up artificial barriers between subjects.

Teaching about Soil, Rocks, and Topography

What happens if you dig a big hole in the middle of an island? It might sink! At least that's what many children believe. A common misconception among primary schoolers is that islands float, just like a boat. Another often seen discrepancy has to do with the way we draw maps. North is almost always "up" and everybody knows that water flows downhill—and, therefore, south. Familiarity with maps of the United States showing the Mississippi River flowing down from the north just adds to the strength of the belief. Try to point out a few rivers (like the Nile in Africa) that flow from south to north. One of the better hands-on exercises is to let children make their own miniature terrain maps of clay in an aluminum pie plate. You won't need to suggest that they include a few mountains, there will usually be mountains galore, mostly in the center of the plate (maybe even a volcano!). Make sure that there are a few low mountains so that when you add water they will become (nonfloating) islands. Let the children sprinkle a few rainstorms in the central mountains to show that rivers flow downhill and away from the mountains, but not necessarily south. Children have great fun with this experiment, just make sure they clean up! (As an extra activity, you can have children use toothpicks to scratch in "shorelines" on the clay as they add more and more water. Show them a topographic map of your area and suddenly all the little lines on it will make sense to them!)

Some children at this age have already started rock collections. Their criteria for selecting rocks vary greatly. Sometimes it has to do with the color, or the "pretty little freckles," or where they were found. Depending on your location, you can have your class bring in as many different small, unusual stones as they can. You can teach them about how the way a stone forms affects its appearance. Show them some of the minerals that are present, even the ones in the speckles (or is that "freckles?"). Talk about how people use these minerals. They can make their own crystals by dissolving alum in an insulated container of hot water. Over the course of a day, sizable crystals will form. They can compare their shape to that of salt, quartz, or ice crystals. Maybe you could make some real "rock" candy from a saturated sugar solution. Another, not nearly so tasty experiment, is to have children mix up sand, soil, and fine gravel with water in a sturdy jar. Let them vigorously shake it and let the different parts settle. This would be a good time to show them photographs of road cutaways (and outcroppings) along an interstate highway. They'll quickly relate the layered rocks to their settling experiment.

Understanding the Oceans

This is one area where it might actually be a good idea to encourage children to watch television. There seems to be more good documentaries about the ocean than about any other science topic. This might be because of the work of people like Jacques Cousteau or maybe it's because of the beautiful colors and mystery of the sea. Whatever the reason, take advantage of some of the excellent shows. Perhaps you can assign a program for homework or maybe you can bring in a videotape. If your school does not have any tapes on hand, you can rent them from your local video store for not much more than a dollar.

Try visiting a local aquarium or pet store. Saltwater aquaria are beautiful, but probably too difficult to maintain in an elementary school setting. Children love watching seahorses, lionfish, starfish, and the colorful clownfish with their anemones. A freshwater aquarium, while not as colorful as the marine variety, can quite easily be set up in the classroom and will act as the source of many science lessons.

Besides observing and perhaps maintaining a log of aquarium observations, children may investigate birth and death of fish (and snails); feeding behaviors; the aquarium as an ecosystem; and the effects of water, light, and temperature on this ecosystem. Set up a simple aquarium—it's worth it!

Studying the Changing Earth

Remember the earlier example exercise with the clay in the pie tin? Well, a similar activity lets children make mountains the same way the earth does. They can even cause earthquakes. The children again work with clay. Only this time, give them several different colors. Have them roll it out into thin, flat pieces. When they place these layers of different colored clay on top of each other (like lasagna) they'll make the connection to the rock layers you've shown them in photographs (and those roadside outcroppings). Now comes the fun part. Tell the children to slowly and carefully push in on the sides of their stack of clay. The hardest part is keeping them from pushing too hard and just mashing everything up. Tell them to be gentle and they should begin to see a few "mountains" forming. If they push one side of the clay away from them while pulling the opposite side toward them, they might actually cause a clayquake! If the clay is stiff enough, a fault (large crack) will form. There are lots of photographs from the LANDSAT satellites (available through NASA; Educational Affairs Division, NASA Headquarters—see reference), which can be used to show students the real thing for comparison. The key in all these exercises is to give the children hands-on experience. They will relate much better to that than to abstract discussions of the same topics.

THE UNIVERSE

Our Solar System

Contrary to what many children believe, the sun is a hot ball of gases. It probably does not have a solid surface. Not only is it a star, but it is a fairly mediocre one! Many children think of it as something special, the only one in the universe. Tell them that this is not the case. Our sun is a middle-aged, middle-sized, absolutely average star. There are millions, if not billions, just like it. Be very sure to warn your students not to look directly at the sun. If they want to do some solar observations (for example, to look for sunspots or to follow the course of an eclipse) poke a pinhole in an index card. Let the sun shine through that hole onto another card held a foot or so away. They will be able to clearly see the disk of the sun on the second card. Most children are surprised at how well this works and how easy it is to do. They love to go home and show their family and friends.

A good project that helps children get an intuitive feeling for the solar system is to let them make a scale model outside. You'll need lots of rocm. Not only do they quickly discover that most of the solar system is empty space, but they also get lots of practice looking up information in reference books and doing conversion calculations. Try to have them scale not only distances from the sun to the planets but also the sizes of the planets themselves. (They won't be able to use the same scale for both. Either the planets would be reasonably sized with the entire model solar system being literally miles across, or the solar system can be scaled to fit into your school yard by making the planets appear as tiny dots! If you have access to a videodisc player, the "Visual Almanac" disc has a nice, properly scaled solar system model laid out along a desert road.) If you can get some of the NASA pictures of the planets, you can have the children make a very eye-catching bulletin board. Be prepared for comments if they have already made the scale model; they'll probably complain that the sizes on the bulletin board display aren't realistic!

SCIENCE ACTIVITY TO TRY

SCALE THE SOLAR SYSTEM

Title: Scale the Solar System

Skills: Measuring, observing, inferring, classifying

Content: Solar system, planets, planet relative sizes, planet distances from the sun

Materials: Different colored construction paper and yarn or string, metric rulers, chalk and magic markers

Procedure: Take the class outside of the building, outside in the hall, or visit the gymnasium for this activity. First, divide the children into teams of two or three students each. Each team will construct a planet (or the sun). Using the scale of 1 mm = 1,000 km, prepare the sun and planets by cutting different colored construction paper circles to the diameters of these celestial bodies based on the following information:

Solar System Scales (Scale: 1 mm = 1,000 km)

Celestial Body	Actual Size (km)	Scale of Diameter (mm)
Mercury	5,000	5
Venus	12,300	12
Earth	2,600	13
Mars	6,700	7
Jupiter	138,700	139
Saturn	114,600	115
Uranus	51,200	51
Neptune	49,600	50
Pluto	5,800	6
Sun	1, 382, 400	1,382
Moon	4,000	4

Tape the large (1,382 mm) yellow circle (sun) to one end of the hall or gym. Label it "sun." Use appropriate-sized circles (by using the chalk and string as a compass and the metric ruler) of different colors to represent the planets. Use the magic markers to label the planets. You might want to decorate the planets. Use the metric ruler to measure the following distances from the sun:

Planet	Distance
Mercury	40 cm
Venus	70 cm
Earth	1.0 m
Mars	1.5 m
Jupiter	5.2 m
Saturn	9.5 m
Uranus	19.6 m
Neptune	30.0 m
Pluto	39.4 m

Closure: What is beyond our solar system?

The scale of the sun and planets and distances apart can make an interesting school display. Although the size of planets and distances in space are practically incomprehensible to children, this activity will help them get a tiny glimpse of the vastness of our solar system and universe.

From seeing movies, children might have lots of ideas about alien creatures that live on other planets. Ask them about the conditions required for life and what things are like on the other planets of our solar system. They'll have to do a little library research or refer to their science textbook. Also mention that scientists are just now finding evidence of planets orbiting far away stars. We don't know if those planets support life. Many scientists would not be surprised if at least a few were inhabited. Asking the children how scientists can determine how there might be planets so far away (when they can only see the central star) can lead to some interesting discussions and maybe even a demonstration of two children holding onto a rope, spinning around each other!

Ask your students if the moon and stars are ever out in the daytime. Younger students almost invariably say no. Older children probably will have seen at least the moon in daytime. They might also realize that the sun is a star. Most have unclear notions about the planets. A very bright star near the horizon in the direction of the setting or rising sun has a good chance of actually being a planet, not a star. All children have seen the moon, but it is very surprising that they know very little about how the phases of the moon happen. Perhaps a short demonstration with a beach ball (or inflatable globe) and light source will show them that reflected sunlight shows off different lunar parts at different times. It is such an easy thing to do and yet can clear up many misunderstandings.

Planets and their Features

What would it be like to live on Mars? Are there any planets that humans could live on? How do we know what other planets are like? There are many questions you can raise to stimulate study. You may want to encourage a historical approach to the subject. Or, you might try using some of the excellent images now available on slides or videodiscs. Students themselves are bound to come up with many questions. What the planets are like has fascinated people for centuries. Remember that you don't have to have all the answers. Direct students to good sources and also let them know that we don't know all we would like to about the solar system. That might be something they could pursue when they grow up!

Beyond the Planets

Children often enjoy learning to recognize the patterns of stars in the sky. A nice activity is to have different groups poke holes into sheets of black paper — making their favorite constellations. After cutting the end off a cylindrical oatmeal box, each group places the end of their box on top of their star map and tapes the paper to it. Turn off the classroom lights and place a flashlight inside the box and they have their own personal planetarium. Each group can try to figure out which constellations other groups created. Sky maps are a good idea because it is normally difficult to get the class together after dark on a clear night to see the real thing. But if you know that the weather will be suitable, assign an examination of the night sky as homework. Many newspapers publish star maps for the area. The nice thing about these publications is that they usually also point out some interesting astronomical phenomenon like a planetary conjunction or meteor shower that your students might be able to observe.

One problem with the aforementioned homemade planetarium is that it tends to perpetuate a mistaken impression children have about the location of stars. Most people think that the stars in any given constellation are somehow related or clustered together. Actually they are not. It is an optical illusion. The distance from the earth to the individual stars in any particular constellation can vary enormously. They only look adjacent because they are nearly in the same direction from us. You might want to make a three- dimensional model of a familiar constellation like the Big Dipper by sticking pins into a sheet of Styrofoam or cardboard. Stick the pins in unevenly. You'll need data on the distance to the stars from the earth. (If you want to, you can glue tiny stars to the heads of the pins to make them more visible.) Mark a big arrow indicating the earth's vantage point. Children looking at the "stars" from this direction will see the familiar pattern. By shifting their view to the side, they'll discover that things aren't quite as they first thought!

The movement of stars and planets across the sky is news to most children. When you think about it, when are they ever allowed to stay up long enough to really see the apparent circling of the stars around Polaris, the North Star? After explaining how this works (the movement of the earth as it turns on its axis makes the stars seem to move through the sky around a point called the celestial north pole, which is directly above the earth's north pole; the North Star is so close to the celestial north pole that it does not seem to move at all), show them some star trail photographs (available from NASA). An interesting thing to do is to ask them how the North Star is special. Once they decide that it is really only a matter of its location, ask them to think about how ancient people might have explained how their compasses (actually lodestones or "lead stones") always seemed to point at that one star. This gets them thinking about how people invent stories to explain what they don't really understand. Ask them how this process is different from science.

Since they probably have only seen pictures or drawings, most children's impressions of what meteors and comets are like are a bit confused. They sometimes think that a meteor trail remains visible for some time while a comet flashes rapidly across the sky, its tail dragging behind like the exhaust gases of a rocket. This is just the reverse of what actually happens. Because of the name, students often think of a meteor as a falling star and that it represents a whole star that slips out of place somehow. Just having children quickly rub their hands together conveys an idea of how friction might make the meteor get so hot that it glows.

Meteor showers are quite common, yet most children have not witnessed the experience. There are two primary reasons why most children have not seen a meteor. First, watching for meteors requires patience! Many children aren't able to (or at least don't want to) keep their attention focused skyward for the amount of time necessary to make it likely that they will actually see a meteor. Second, the best time to watch for meteors is after midnight. Even if they are allowed to stay up that late, what are the chances that they'll be able to keep looking up at the sky without getting drowsy?

Students are sometimes surprised to find that meteors can hit the earth, leaving craters, just like on the moon. Show them a photograph of the famous meteor crater in Arizona. If you can visit a museum, you might be able to show them actual meteorites. It's fun to talk about where they might come from and how old they might be.

LOOKING BACK

In this chapter, we have looked at some different ways of involving children with learning about their surroundings, both near and far. As we found in Chapter 5 about life science, children accumulate a lot of ideas before they ever get to your classroom. In the case of the earth and the universe, some of their thoughts are hazy and incomplete. You will probably have less difficulty getting them to change their conceptions of the earth and universe because they aren't as sure about what they know about them. With the beauty found in astronomical photographs and the sudden insight at the simplicity of how day changes into night and winter into spring, you might inspire more than a passing interest in science.

SELF-TEST

- Discuss a misconception or two that children have about the earth and the universe. How could hands-on/minds-on science teaching help change these naive ideas?

- What causes rain?

- Childrens' discrepancies with maps are intriguing. Where do you think—north is almost always "up", and water flows downhill and therefore south—might have originated?

- Think of a method that would allow you to cause "earthquakes" in your classroom.

- Construct a personal planetarium as described on p. 118. Devise an imaginary constellation. What is its name and shape and story?

- Why does it appear that the North star stands still?

SCOPE AND SEQUENCE

Once again, we suggest a possible scope and sequence of topics. This is not carved in granite. Feel free to adjust coverage and order as you see fit.

Kindergarten   Seasons, conservation, temperature, the earth

First grade   Landforms, oceans, atmosphere, kinds of weather, seasons, sun, moon, stars

Second grade   Atmosphere, oceans, changing weather, stars

Third grade   Geology, soil, volcanoes, earthquakes, storms, clouds, sun, moon, planets

Fourth grade   Changing landforms, oceans, solar system, phases of the moon

Fifth grade   Earth's crust, climates, constellations, gravity

Sixth grade   Plate tectonics, energy resources, weather forecasting

REFERENCES FROM RESEARCH

Gunstone, R. and White, R. (1981). Understanding of gravity. *Science Education,* 65(3), 291–299.

Hashweh, M. (1988). Descriptive studies of students' conceptions in science. *Journal of Research in Science Teaching,* 25(2), 121–134.

Nussbaum, J. and Novick, S. (1976). An assessment of children's concepts of the earth utilizing structured interviews. *Science Education,* 60, 535–550.

Sadler, P. (1987, July). *Misconceptions in astronomy.* Proceedings of the Second International Seminar on Misconceptions and Educational Strategies in Science and Mathematics, Ithaca, N.Y.: Cornell University, pp. 422–425.

PRACTICAL RESOURCES

Hardy, G. and Tolman, M. (1991). Cakequake: an earth-shaking experience. *Science and Children,* 29(1),18–21.

Philips, W. (1991). Earth science misconceptions. *The Science Teacher,* February, 21–23.

Geological survey maps of areas west of the Mississippi can be obtained from the Geological Survey Distribution Section, Federal Center, Denver, CO 80225

Geological survey maps of areas east of the Mississippi can be obtained from the Washington Distribution Section, U.S. Geological Survey,1200 S. Eads Street, Arlington, VA 22202

Educational Affairs Division, NASA Headquarters, Washington, DC 20546, can supply a wealth of wonderful materials.

The Visual Almanac videodisc is available from Optical Data Corporation, 30 Technology Drive, Warren, NJ 07059.

Tolman, M. and Morton, J. (1986). *Earth science activities for grades 2–8*. W. Nyack, N.Y.: Parker Publishing Co., Inc.

CHAPTER

7 Teaching Children about Heat, Light, and Sound

LOOKING AHEAD

The material covered in the next few pages is mostly from an area of science called physics. (You might want to mention this fact to your students in an effort to "immunize" them against the fear of the subject that often develops as the children go through school.) As we found in earlier chapters, science concepts surround children as they grow and function in the world. The three areas of physics dealt with in this chapter—heat, light, and sound—have many real-life examples to which children can relate. Beyond this, without much special equipment, teachers can create some rather spectacular demonstrations that are not only engaging but also help students grasp the material more fully. We'll look at several of these in the pages ahead.

CAN YOU?

- Explain what heat, light and sound are? They are fascinating, integral parts of our lives, but what are they?

- Explain the difference between heat and temperature?

- Suggest how you would teach the difference between heat and temperature to children?

- Suggest some of the misconceptions children have with the concepts of heat, light and sound? How might you approach teaching to change these misconceptions?

- Plan to incorporate the problems approach into an instructional unit on heat and temperature?

- Combine some of the topics dealt with in this chapter with another area of science; for example, life science?

HEAT

Misconceptions about Heat

Children and most adults have some rather serious misunder-standings of the concepts of heat and temperature. Most people simply don't realize that the two ideas are quite different. Temperature is just a number from some arbitrarily constructed scale. We are most familiar with the Fahrenheit and Celsius scales, but there are others. The Fahrenheit scale has its zero point at about the melting point of a salt and ice mixture. The 100° point is approximately the temperature of the human body. The Celsius scale was originally called the Centigrade scale because there were 100 gradations or degrees between the freezing and boiling points of water. Nonetheless, these numbering systems and calibration points are entirely arbitrary. There is no magic in them other than that they can be readily created for ease in calibrating new thermometers.

Heat, however, is nothing more or less than a form of energy. Temperature scales have been designed so that heat energy flows from objects with higher temperatures to objects with lower temperatures. This close connection between heat and energy is the source of the misconception. In most cases, adding heat energy to an object raises its temperature while removing heat energy makes its temperature go down. This does not always happen, though. Have students carefully measure the temperature of a very well-stirred beaker of ice water as it sits on an electric hot plate. Any heat added to the beaker must first melt the ice before the temperature can go up. If the students measure the temperature while the ice is melting (and everything is very well stirred) they will find the temperature holds at 0°C. Once all the ice is gone, the temperature starts to rise. The point of this exercise may escape students unless you carefully point out what the heat energy is doing. (They tend to think that it just takes a while for things to heat up.) If your students need practice graphing, have them make a graph of temperature versus time in this activity. There will be a plateau while the ice melts, then a fairly straight line at an upward angle as the water temperature rises. The time axis also could be considered an indicator of heat energy added, assuming the beaker is heated uniformly. Having a graph with temperature on the vertical axis and heat energy on the horizontal axis helps students in the upper elementary grades recognize the difference between the two concepts.

Another area where many children experience difficulty because of naive understanding concerns the use of insulating materials to reduce the flow of heat out of a warm object. This mostly is the result of their own experience. When they get cold, they wrap up in a blanket and quickly feel warmer. The blanket acts as if it were a source of heat. Some children may believe that the blanket acts as a shield keeping cold air away from them, which is true. The key point is that the air trapped in the blanket helps reduce the flow of heat energy out of their bodies. If you can bring in an electric blanket or heating pad and contrast how it works with how a regular blanket works, you might begin to change their misconception. Be prepared; "Habits of the mind are hard to break!"

Molecular Motion: The Inside Story on Heat

Ask a scientist what heat is all about and he or she will probably start talking about molecular vibrations. This means that the molecules inside an object shake faster when heat energy is added. The reason an object cools is because the molecules of which it is made start to slow down. (Absolute zero, nearly -460°F, would be the complete absence of molecular vibrations, a state that can be approached but never quite reached.) When children quickly rub their hands together, the friction between the two surfaces causes molecules in their skin to vibrate faster and the children feel the heat. Children readily understand how a microwave oven works when they find out that the special waves make any water molecules inside the food vibrate, making the food warmer. It is almost like heating by friction, only from the inside. Things without much water, like a paper plate, don't heat up, but a moist hot dog resting on the plate does. This type of heating is much more efficient than that of conventional ovens, which must first transfer heat energy from a gas flame or electrical element to the air and then to the food. Try the following activity, which will show fourth-grade children that the faster the molecules of a substance are moving, the hotter that material will get.

SCIENCE ACTIVITY TO TRY

HOT, COLD, FAST, AND SLOW MOVING MOLECULES

Title: Hot, Cold, Fast, and Slow Moving Molecules

Skills: Observing, inferring, predicting, hypothesizing, using variables

Content: Temperature, hot, cold, molecular motion

Materials: For each team of two or three children: two clear glasses, red and blue food coloring, two eye droppers, hot and cold water

Procedure: Have the teams pick up the equipment and then fill one glass half full with very cold water and another with hot tap water. Fill the two eye droppers with the two food colorings (one dropper with red food coloring and one with blue). Have the children predict what will happen when the food colorings are put into the glasses of water. Put 6 to 7 drops of food coloring into the separate glasses of water at exactly the same time. Observe what happens in each container. Compare the movement of color in each glass. In which container did the color spread more rapidly? Perhaps try food coloring with other, different water temperatures (use a thermometer) and record the results.

Closure: How does the temperature of the water affect the speed of the food-coloring molecules?

With younger students, you can start them thinking by asking questions such as, "What is heat?" "How do we use heat?" or "Where do we get heat?" They will probably ask about fevers. You might also want to bring up how shivering makes them warmer. (Muscles are active and contract or tighten, which, in turn, helps to increase our body temperature.) The importance of warm clothing in cold weather can be talked about, bringing other health topics into the discussion. Using thermometers to record the indoor and outdoor temperature is an important skill for children in the earlier grades to acquire. Calibrating thermometers is a fun task, but, with any experiment involving heat energy, you need to stress the importance of safety. Something as simple as starting with a beaker of ice cubes to calibrate the freezing point, melting them into water, and then boiling the water (boiling point) can be a fascinating exercise when observations are carefully noted and discussed.

Understanding Heat Capacity

A common question arises when children begin caring for plants or animals in the classroom: "Are they going to be okay?" As an example of how you can be receptive to children's ideas and yet still keep to your science program or syllabus, let's take a look at how a teacher is able to turn this biology-oriented concern into a lesson on heat.

Ms. Roberts: Our new aquarium is all set up. The guppies look okay. We just fed them and made sure the air pump is running. Is there anything else we should think about before going home for the weekend?

Juan: Won't they get hungry? Are you coming in to feed them?

David: Remember that we shouldn't feed them too much. The woman in the pet store said that once every two or three days would be okay.

Juan: They'll get lonely, though! Don't fish get lonely, Ms. Roberts?

Ms. Roberts: Well, I hadn't really thought about that. Do you know of any examples of fish that like to be with other fish?

Delilah: Yeah! Sometimes they swim around in schools. Remember in the video we saw whole bunches of them.

Juan: That's right! I'm afraid they'll be lonely or get cold or something over the weekend.

Ms. Roberts: Well, we can't do much about the loneliness, but we could monitor the temperature to see what happens while we aren't here. How would we do that?

Diana: Do we have to come in on Saturday and Sunday? I don't think my parents will let me.

Juan: I'll come in. I don't mind! That way they won't be lonely either!

Ms. Roberts: That's nice of you, Juan. But I don't think kids are supposed to be in the building when it is officially closed. We need some way to record the temperature, even if no one is here.

Diana: We can have the computer do it, can't we? We have those thermometer things. Remember when we graphed the temperature of water and stuff?

Ms. Roberts: Good idea! I think we can adjust the computer program so that it records the temperature once an hour for a couple of days. We should have time to set it up before the bell rings. Let's try it!

It may not seem like much of this conversation dealt with teaching children the difference between heat and temperature. That's true. But it set the stage by creating a situation where the concepts could be examined and the children would be highly interested in the results. The real discussion will happen next Monday morning when the children look at the graphs of the temperature of the room and the water over the weekend.

Juan: Hey, look! The water didn't change nearly as much as the room did. The water didn't get much below 15° [Celsius] even though the room was down to 12°. How come?

Ms. Roberts: It looks like the air in the room was a lot more sensitive to the loss of heat energy than the water in the aquarium was.

Diana: But shouldn't all the heat from the warm water go into the room? Why aren't they the same temperature?

Ms. Roberts: Take a look at the graph of the water temperature over the weekend. Do you see how it keeps going down? What do you suppose would happen if we kept on watching the temperature for a couple more days?

Billy: It would probably just keep going down, wouldn't it?

Ms. Roberts: How low would the temperature go?

Diana: Till it's at the same temperature as the room!

Ms. Roberts: Right, because heat energy flows from higher temperature areas to lower temperature. [Pauses a few seconds.] Now, why didn't the water temperature drop down as fast as the air temperature? [wait-time]Compare the water graph with the air one.

Juan: I don't get it. It's not insulated. I mean the water is just sitting there in the air. The glass isn't gonna slow the heat down that much . . . besides the whole top of the water is touching the air anyhow.

Ms. Roberts: Good point, Juan. There must be something else that we haven't thought about yet. Does anyone know what it might be? [Long pause, again, wait-time.] Juan, do you remember what I said when you asked why the water didn't cool down from 15° to 12°?

Juan: No.

Ms. Roberts: I said that it looked like the air was a lot more sensitive to the loss of heat energy than the water was. Different substances react differently to adding or removing heat. Some of them, like air, change temperature a lot. Others, like water, are less sensitive and so only change their temperature a little when you add or remove heat energy. Think about turning on the burner of an electric stove. Does the it take very long for the air above the burner to get hot?

Juan and Diana: NO!

Ms. Roberts: Now, let's say you put a pan of water on the stove. Does it get hot as quickly as the air?

Diana: It takes a long time. My mom says a watched pot never boils!

Juan: You mean if you keep looking at a pot of water it won't start to boil? I don't believe it! Can we try it, Ms. Roberts?

Ms. Roberts: I'm sure we can. We'll have to be careful around the hot plate. We don't want anyone to get burned. Remember what we are investigating . . . we are looking at how slow water is to change temperature. Are there any other things [variables] we have to control, or is there something we should systematically change to see what happens?

This class is well on its way to a careful examination of the topic of heat capacity. Ms. Roberts has some other experiments in mind and even some examples about how differing heat capacities affect the weather in their area. She likes to teach real-life science.

Heat Moving from Place to Place

We saw in the last vignette that children can grasp some of the important ideas behind heat energy transfer from one place to another. Children usually have little trouble learning how to discern whether heat is traveling by conduction (transfer of heat from one molecule to another; i.e., the flow of heat from the warm end of a metal rod to the cool end), convection (transfer of heat by movement of fluids; i.e., hot water spreading into a container of cooler water), or radiation (transfer of heat energy by waves; i.e., warming yourself on a sunny day). They are usually a little concerned to hear the word *radiation*, equating it to nuclear radiation. You should mention this point, even if none of the students brings it up. Someone in the class is bound to be thinking it and, if not corrected, students can really get confused. Ask them how the heat from the sun reaches the earth. This is a good question after already discussing conduction and convection, both of which require some kind of material to support the movement of heat energy. When asked about the sun, children will quickly realize that sunshine is what brings the heat to use. You can tell them that sunlight is not only light they can see, but it also has light in it that their eyes cannot see. Some of that light is heat.

Heat Causing Expansion of Objects

There are thousands of examples of thermal expansion joints built into things around us. Once children know what to look for, they'll suddenly understand why bridges have those funny interlocking teeth at each end. Brick walls have long vertical joints that look like mortar joints, but have a softer material in them. The workings of thermometers make more sense all of a sudden. Now children will be able to tell their parents how to get a stuck jar lid off by running hot water over it! Watch out for problems when looking at the expansion of ice as it freezes, however. Water is a very unusual substance. Almost everything else contracts as it cools. (Water does, too, at least until it is close to its freezing point, but after freezing it expands.) Don't let this strange behavior distract students from the normal response of other substances to heat energy.

Planning a Unit on Heat and Temperature

Shifting gears a bit, this text, so far, has given you isolated activity lesson plans to try with your students. Let's take a look at how to cover a science topic in depth over a number of weeks; this is called a science unit! Anytime you start thinking about how to teach a particular topic, start by considering what the children already "know." Earlier in this chapter, we discussed some of the misconceptions children hold about heat and temperature. To refresh your memory, youngsters (and adults) confuse the two concepts. Children also have a hard time understanding heat transfer. They tend to misunderstand how a blanket works. They will realize that it can keep them warm, but not recognize that a blanket will also slow down the melting of an ice cube in a warm room. It is an insulator.

So how do you go about determining what children think about the topic you are going to be teaching them? It's simple—just ask them! It may take a little careful probing to disclose fuzzy ideas. (Children often say "I don't know" even when they have some thoughts about a subject.) You have to walk a fine line between listening for misconceptions and not damaging their self-esteem. Remember that at this point you are purposely trying to *uncover* mistaken ideas, not correct them. Besides, just telling a student he or she is wrong about something doesn't guarantee that the correct ideas will replace the old concepts. That kind of change can only be made by the child. After a few years of teaching you will find that each class of students has very similar ideas. This will make it easier to plan in advance for ways of addressing the problems.

To carry out this sort of diagnostic approach in the classroom, you have several options. Probably the least threatening to students to is talk to them individually about the topic and what they know about it. Another approach is to list on the board or flipchart children's different ideas. Have a brainstorming session! This can be more productive if the classroom atmosphere is such that the students feel free to speak their minds and even make mistakes. This is something that takes time to develop, but it is worthwhile. Treat the beginning of each new science topic as a brainstorming session, listing everyone's ideas as quickly as you can. Not only does this create a nice list of initial concepts for your use, it also focuses the students' attention and helps them sort out what they feel about a topic. Consider the following:

Ms. Ortega: OK, class, just like I promised, it's brainstorming time!

Many students: Yea!

Ms. Ortega: All right, I need some ideas about heat and temperature. We are going to be studying it next week, and I need to know what you already have figured out about it. Who's first? Hector?

Hector: Ya measure temperature on a thermometer!

Ms. Ortega [quickly writing the idea on the board]: OK. Another? Sally?

Sally: It's hotter in the summer than in the winter.

Ms. Ortega [again writing]: Fine. Next? Joey?

Joey: Uh . . . You have a temperature when you're sick.

Ms. Ortega [writes idea on board]: Uh huh. Who's next?

Susan: My Dad says we need to insulate our house to keep the heat in.

Ms. Ortega: Can you make a statement about heat and insulation?

Susan: Yeah! Insulation keeps heat in.

Ms. Ortega [writes the idea on the board and waits a few moments]: Any other ideas? What do you do if your body is cold?

Bryan: Put on a coat!

Ms. Ortega: What does that do for you?

Bryan: It warms you up.

Ms. Ortega: How about a statement?

Bryan: A coat makes you warmer.

Ms. Ortega [puts it on the board]: OK. How's our list look so far? Anyone else have an idea they want to put up here? (wait-time)

Do you see how the teacher wrote the ideas down in a non-threatening, nonjudgmental way? You have to be careful not to encourage the correct ideas at this point, mainly because the students can also detect you discouraging their misconceptions and they might be less willing to share them. Did you also notice the general attitude of the students to the session? They enjoyed it. Brainstorming can be fun if people feel free to express as many ideas as they can, in a rapid-fire manner.

What did the children's responses indicate about their initial understanding of heat and temperature? Not surprisingly, students didn't really differentiate between the two ideas. They mixed in the idea of a fever with the general concept of temperature. They knew insulation is used to "hold heat in" but probably thought it was an all or nothing thing, not recognizing that insulation only slows the flow of heat. The idea that a coat acts as a source of heat may be hidden in Bryan's reply. As is typical with naive conceptions, the ideas are not clear cut.

Now it's time to begin thinking of ways to address the misconceptions. The main idea behind the problems approach to science teaching is to develop a set of leading questions (or a strategy for drawing these questions out of students). You might want to have a freewheeling session similar to the preceding brainstorming time. Call it "What do you want to know about the topic?" or "Question Brainstorming" time. To find the answer to questions, both the teacher and the students must be prepared for some work. The teacher (and students) comes up with interesting and revealing situations to examine. These tasks should directly challenge students to consider their own ideas about the topic of study and help them change their naive conceptions, if necessary. Hopefully, the tasks or activities will be interesting enough to motivate further study and memorable enough to make a lasting impression.

Now let's try a three- to four-week unit on heat and temperature for third graders. First, review the first part of this chapter. Consult a science textbook (if there is one!) from your elementary science classroom and look at one of the many new science activity resource books on the market (many have been listed in the Practical Resources sections in this book). Try to write up a unit that includes the following important components:

- Title

- Rationale

- Bibliography

- Objectives

- Activities

- Teacher background information

- Additional integrated activities

- Evaluation component

- Lesson plans

Take a look at the general methods book in this series if you're not sure about one of the components of your unit.

LIGHT

Properties of Light

The topic of light can be enjoyable, regardless of the grade level of the student. Younger children can be asked questions such as, "What do you know of that gives off light?" They will almost certainly name the sun. (They might also mention the moon – a common misconception; it gives off reflected light from the sun.) With a little encouragement they also will think of things like electric bulbs, fires, chemical glowsticks, and even fireflies. See if they can classify different lights by color or brightness, whether it blinks, or whatever categories they can devise. Try asking them to draw a picture of themselves standing outside reading a sign. Let them trace the path of light from the sun to the sign and then to their eyes. A common belief (and one that was held by scientists up to the time of Newton whatever is being looked at. So make sure your students' drawings show which way the light is going.

This problem of remembering which way light travels can often be helped by letting young students work with shadows. They can use sunlight or a desk lamp or slide projector as a light source. From these experiments they can quickly learn that light travels in straight lines. Multiple light sources can be used to create some mystery patterns that they can decipher.

As a way of incorporating the study of light into other science areas, have children study the eye's response to varying brightness. One student can watch another child's eyes as they read a book in strong light. By shading the reader's eyes with a hand, the observer will see the friend's pupils quickly expanding and then contracting again once he or she removes the hand. But be sure to caution students not to shine a bright light into anyone's eyes or to look directly at bright lights.

Making Rainbows

You shouldn't be too surprised to discover that children love to make their own rainbows. You can pick the method that is best for that particular day. If it's a warm, sunny day a simple garden hose can be used outside to create a spray in the sunlight. This might be best done as a demonstration by the teacher instead of an experiment by the students! By careful observation children can discover that the rainbow moves when they move (the arc stays centered on the shadow of their head) and that red is on the outside of the bow. This last point can be turned into a detective game. Without too much effort, children can locate drawings of "broken" rainbows. Some artists never seemed to learn the proper ordering of colors—remember Roy G. Biv—or that red is the outer color. Children enjoy finding the errors in magazines and in their own books and toys.

If an outdoor rainbow isn't possible, you can make an indoor version with a cake pan filled with water. Just place a mirror so that one end is supported by the edge of the pan while the other end lays on the bottom of the pan. Shine a flashlight through the water onto the mirror and you'll have a rainbow on the ceiling. If you want to avoid water completely, use a glass prism and, after shining light through it, teach the children that it is pronounced *prism*, not prison!

It can be interesting to ask the children why black and white are not part of the rainbow. Stress that they are not actually colors, just the absence or presence of light.

Looking at the Optical Properties of Matter

Youngsters can categorize materials you give them as either transparent, translucent, or opaque. Older students might enjoy working with convex and concave lenses or colored filters. A collection of glass or plastic lenses lets children not only explore their effect on the light passing through them, they can also learn to use them as a tool for close examination. You might want to ask an optometrist or ophthalmologist for a few old glasses to show students how they work to correct near- or farsightedness.

Many children think that only glass mirrors reflect light, so be sure that they get a chance to play with some soup spoons. Try to get them to understand the difference between the reflection we see from a shiny surface and the light that reflects from all objects so that we can see them.

Scattering of light by tiny particles can be demonstrated by shining a flashlight through an aquarium filled with water and a few drops of milk. Students will be able to see the light beam as a slightly bluish cylinder in the water. Hold a piece of white paper at the side of the aquarium so that light travels through the milky water, out the side of the aquarium, and onto the paper. Children will see a somewhat reddish circle of light. This is the time to start talking about blue skies and red sunsets. They'll have a whole new understanding of these daily phenomena when they realize that they see a red sunset only because somebody else has a blue sky! That brings up the often-asked question, "What makes the sky blue?" (Sunlight is scattered as it strikes our atmosphere. Air molecules absorb some of the light and re-radiate it out in all directions. This works best with bluish light since its wavelength somehow "fits" best with the molecules in the air. The blue light gets scattered in all directions while the rest of the spectrum—mostly red—goes straight through. Looking up into the sky allows one to see the blue light that gets scattered toward the ground.)

The Electromagnetic Spectrum

The full electromagnetic spectrum can be difficult for children to understand because they can only see a small part of it. There are several ways of addressing this problem. Some teachers begin by pointing out that our eyes are only sensitive to something called the visible spectrum, but our skin can detect the infrared or heat portion. They then discuss detectors for other parts of the electromagnetic spectrum—things like TVs, radios, radar antennas, X-ray film, or even microwave oven testers. Another approach is to discuss the different parts of the spectrum as having different amounts of energy. Radio waves carry a little energy, visible light has more, ultraviolet even more (it can damage our skin by causing sunburn), X rays have so much that they can penetrate the skin, and gamma rays have so much that they usually go completely through skin and bones. To demonstrate the energy contained in microwaves bring in a small oven unit and make some popcorn! Ask the question, How do microwaves make this happen?

Mixing Colors by Addition and Subtraction

You can start a discussion of light mixing by assigning a homework problem: "What color are the dots that make up a color television screen?" (red, green, and blue). When you are discussing the results, ask the children why a snowstorm during a TV program can appear white when there are no white dots. A very effective demonstration is to use three slide projectors and some red, green, and blue filters. By shining the light from each projector through a filter and having the three different color beams strike the same surface, a white patch becomes visible. This makes it very clear what white light is (it contains all colors) and how different colors can be formed by the addition of colored light. You can either leave it at that or explain why it works that way by referring to the different color sensitivities of the cone cells in the retina. (Cone cells in the retina help us recognize different colors. Cone cells are sensitive to either red, green, or blue light. When real white light consisting of all the colors hits our eyes, all three types of cones are stimulated. The brain interprets that as white. When a television screen sends out just red, green, and blue light it also stimulates those three kinds of cones, fooling the brain into thinking there is white light hitting the eye.)

After children have seen the addition of light, ask them what will happen if they color the same area of a piece of paper using red, green, and blue crayons. Have them try it. They'll know in advance that the result won't be white. They will probably remember putting yellow and blue together to get green. This color subtraction process can cause a great deal of confusion if you don't carefully explain what colors of light are absorbed and what colors are reflected from different crayon pigments. If an object absorbs all the colors that strike it, then it can't reflect light. As a result, it appears black. If it absorbs none of the colors and reflects all of them, the object appears white. Most objects are somewhere in between—absorbing some colors and reflecting other colors. In our examples, the red color absorbs all other colors. Thus, if red is mixed with green, the red absorbs the green. The green, in turn, absorbs the red. As a result, the colors absorb each other and the mixture looks black! Now try this activity with your second graders!

SCIENCE ACTIVITY TO TRY

MIXING COLORS

Title: Mixing Colors

Skills: Observing, predicting, classifying, recording data, hypothesizing

Content: Colors, absorption of light, combinations of colors

Materials: Various colors of tempera paint, white construction paper, paint brushes, containers of water, paper towels

Procedure: Divide the class into teams of two or four students each and begin by listing the available paints (colors) on the board. Ask the children to predict what different color combinations will turn out to be; record their predictions on the board. Distribute the equipment and test the predictions (paint different color mixtures on the construction paper). Make new predictions and test them. Form a hypothesis about the formation of black. Experiment!

Have the children put their names on the construction paper. Go back to the class predictions (on the board); discuss their predictions and the results from testing their predictions. Have they observed that when two colors are mixed, a third color is formed? Did they notice that, when mixed together, colors often produce black mixtures but never white? (When mixing pigments, many colors are absorbed, or subtracted, from the spectrum and, because when paints are mixed they tend to absorb light and each other, a mixture of many colors usually results in black.)

Closure: Erase the board. Ask, "Who can tell me what I get when I mix yellow and blue? (green) How about red and yellow? (orange) Red and blue? (purple) What about red, blue, and yellow? (black) Why black?"

If you take the time to make sure your students understand what is going on, they'll have a greater appreciation for something they've been involved with all their lives.

SOUND

The most difficult thing about teaching children about sound is keeping everything under control so people outside the classroom are not subjected to the same lesson! This is an area where you really need to be considerate of others. If you are planning a noisy lesson and weather permits, take your class outside. If the gymnasium or auditorium is available, use it. The music room is often located so that sound inside will not disturb others. Look around or be prepared to maintain firm control over your students as they explore different aspects of sound.

Discussing the Wave Nature of Sound

This might be a good time to talk about waves in general. Children usually can relate to terms like *frequency* (number of vibrations per second) and *amplitude* (size of the sound wave) because they can easily hear the change in a sound as each parameter is changed. Playing with a long spring or slinky can reinforce the concepts. Children enjoy imagining what sound would look like if we could actually see it. (Changing pitch would appear as a changing color, changing loudness would show up as a variation in brightness.) This also requires that they recall what you have taught them about light.

One of the more difficult concepts in understanding waves is that they don't actually result in large-scale movement of matter. (Children often think that water waves actually carry the water along with them as they travel; they don't, they move along through the water.) Discussing sound waves seems to be a good way to attack this misconception. Children are usually willing to recognize the fact that a faraway sound can make a vibration in the air without causing a breeze to blow.

Letting children feel their voice box vibrate gives them an intuitive understanding of sound vibrations. (Have them put their fingers to their throat and hum "zzzzzzzzzzzz.") Homemade kazoos from a comb and wax paper also work well, if you can put up with the impromptu concerts that you can count on happening. If you have your students do this experiment, use either new or sterilized combs. Children like to share their combs, and that is usually not a good idea.

Other musical instruments include rubber-band and shoebox guitars, and water glasses or pop bottles with different amounts of water in them. Ask children to explain why a nearly full bottle gives a high note when you blow across it but a low note when tapped. A nearly empty bottle gives a low note when blown across and a high note when tapped. Have them consider what is vibrating in each case. (When blowing, the air is vibrating, and the nearly empty bottle gives the low note; when struck, the bottle and its contents are vibrating, the larger mass of the nearly full bottle gives the low note.) Try it!

Hearing the Sound of Music

Depending on the grade level, you can count on a few students being able to bring in their real musical instruments. They are usually more than happy to show their friends how they work and how they are tuned. It shouldn't be too hard to convince the music teacher to pay a visit with some other instruments.

If you have access to a computer with the proper software, your students can sample sound from different sources of sound and actually examine the waves. You can stimulate discussion by asking how one can distinguish a guitar from a piano, even when both are playing the same note.

Measuring the Speed of Sound

Students often have experienced the time lag between seeing a distant event (like a hammer hitting a nail) and hearing the sound. During your explanation, don't reinforce the belief that light arrives instantly. Sure, it's fast, but it still takes time. Children who are practicing multiplication can find the time it takes light to reach the earth from the sun by knowing the speed of light (186,000 mi/sec; 300,000 km/sec) and the distance (93,000,000 mi; 149,500,000 km)—a little over 8 minutes. Have them imagine that sound (1,100 ft/sec; 335 m/sec in air) could travel through the emptiness of space. How long would it take sound to travel the same 93 million miles?— over 15 years!

Why do we hear thunder after we see lightning? Teach your students the trick for determining the distance to a lightning flash by counting the delay between seeing and hearing the flash. Dividing by 5 gives you the miles to the storm, dividing by 3 results in kilometers. (Light travels rapidly, but sound travels relatively slowly, moving about 1 mile in 5 seconds (1 km in 3 secs).)

Some of the microcomputer lab packages include the equipment and software needed for your students to accurately measure the speed of sound. If you don't have access to a computer or the sound probes, have them use a stopwatch and tape measure to time an echo of a loud hand clap as it goes to a far building and returns to them. The result won't be accurate to 5 decimal places, but it is fun for them to measure the speed of something as fast as sound waves.

LOOKING BACK

Heat and temperature are unique topics. On the one hand, children readily identify high and low temperatures and the relationship between adding heat energy and the resulting increase in temperature. On the other hand, there is great confusion between the concepts of heat and temperature. One approach to clearing up the misunderstandings is to demonstrate situations where adding heat doesn't cause a change in temperature. You also must deal with misconceptions about sources of heat: "The coat is warm." Light and sound are usually fun to learn about (and to teach about). In all three areas, our suggestion is the same—lots of hands-on activities (keeping safety in mind at all times).

SELF-TEST

- What is the difference between heat and temperature?
- What are some of the misconceptions children have with the concepts of heat, light and sound?
- What does it mean to say that heat travels by conduction, convection or radiation?
- What are some of the parts that make up an instructional unit?
- What are some of the benefits of starting a new science topic with a class brainstorming session?
- What causes a rainbow to occur?
- What makes the sky blue?
- What happens when you mix these colors: yellow and blue? red and yellow? red and blue? red, blue and yellow? Try it!

SCOPE AND SEQUENCE

How would you decide what detail to add to the following suggested list of topics?

Kindergarten   Hot and cold, thermometers, use of heat, recognizing sounds

First grade	Heat energy, shadows, making sounds, musical instruments,
Second grade	Heat versus temperature, transparent, translucent, opaque materials, kinds of sound
Third grade	Heat and matter, expansion and contraction, energy, properties of sound, voice
Fourth grade	Properties of light and sound, matter and light, musical instruments
Fifth grade	Properties of matter, color, sources of heat, light, and sound
Sixth grade	Thermal properties of matter, reflection, refraction, optical instruments

REFERENCES FROM RESEARCH

Anderson, C. and Smith, E. (1983). *Children's conceptions of light and color: developing the concept of unseen rays.* Paper presented at the Annual Meeting of the American Educational Research Association, Montreal, Canada.

Clough, E. and Driver, R. (1985). Secondary students' conceptions of the conduction of heat: bringing together scientific and personal views. *Physics Education,* 20, 177–187.

Erickson, G. (1979). Children's conceptions of heat and temperature. *Science Education,* 63(2), 221–230.

Linn, M. and Songer, N. (1991). Teaching thermodynamics to middle school students: what are appropriate cognitive demands?, *Journal of Research in Science Teaching,* 28, 885–918.

Stary, R. (1990). Children's conception of changes in the state of matter: from liquid (or solid) to gas. *Journal of Research in Science Teaching,* 27(3), 247–266.

Strauss, S. (1983, June). *Engaging children's intuitive physics concepts via curriculum units: the case of heat and temperature.* Proceedings of the International Seminar on Misconceptions and Educational Strategies in Science and Mathematics, Ithaca, N.Y.: Cornell University, pp. 292–303.

PRACTICAL RESOURCES

Lunetta, V. and Novick, S. (1982). *Inquiring and problem-solving in the physical sciences: a sourcebook*. Dubuque, Iowa: Kendall/Hunt.

Tolman, M. and Morton, J. (1986). *Physical science activities for grades 2–8*. W. Nyack, N.Y.: Parker Publishing.

Voyage of the Mimi MBL "Whales and their environment" has a speed-of-sound measurement experiment. It is available from Sunburst Communications, 39 Washington Avenue, Pleasantville, NY 10570-2898, (800) 431–1934.

8 Teaching Children about Machines, Magnetism, and Electricity

LOOKING AHEAD

In this, the last chapter dealing specifically with science content, we will focus some more on physics. In the real world, you may not know it, but you encounter physics examples all the time. We will discuss ways to help children learn about machines, electricity, and magnetism. Interspersed will be some ideas about energy. Some teachers prefer to teach separate lessons on the concept of energy, because it is such an important topic. Others would rather incorporate it into instruction on a variety of topics, because it is involved in just about every concept we teach. Which method do you prefer? Do you think one way is easier for children? How would you go about finding out the answer to these questions?

CAN YOU?

- Think of some of the misconceptions children have about machines, magnetism, and electricity?

- Explain how you keep children from thinking you "get something for nothing" when using a machine? For example, explain how you can easily lift a car (with one hand!) by using a jack.

- Indicate how you can simultaneously explain how many different things electricity does for us while also stressing electrical safety?

MACHINES

Some Difficulties Understanding Machines

Children's misconceptions in this area often arise from the fact that many of the key vocabulary words associated with machines also have casual, non scientific definitions. This, of course, is complicated by the usual tendency for misunderstandings to arise from children's everyday experiences. Let's begin by looking at some of the everyday definitions of scientific terms that can end up confusing children.

Ask a dozen children what "work" is and you'll get twelve different answers. Some think it is the homework that you assign for them to complete before coming back to school the next day. Others know that it is a place where Mommy or Daddy go every morning. Or, perhaps cueing on what they have heard adults say, a few children view work as any unpleasant task. None of these ideas has anything to do with the scientific definition of work. Unfortunately, many science textbooks don't help children make the transition from their intuitive notions that work involves effort to the conception of work as applied force multiplied by distance moved. You will often see a pair of drawings, one showing a child sliding a box or similar object, the other showing someone pushing against a brick wall. The book will point out that work (W) is only done in the first picture since there is both an applied force (F) and a distance (d) moved ($W = F \times d$). This does not fit well with the child's impression that pushing against a wall for a long time would tire them out, even though the wall did not move. (Actually, there is work done inside the muscles, which operate by a series of microscopically sized, repeated contractions. In other words, the distance moved is inside the body, even though the wall is fixed. No work was done on the wall, but energy was expended inside the body. That's why you get tired.)

The concept of energy also can be confusing for children. Rather than promoting impressions of it as some form of personal enthusiasm, tell your students that if they are full of energy, then they will be able to accomplish a lot. They acquire energy by eating food. This can be easily tied into nutrition lessons by noting the importance of eating a good breakfast. Another science focus can review the path energy takes from the sun to plants to food to humans. If you happen to be teaching physical science, very straightforward discussions of how food energy allows children to do physical work are in order. What is important to see is that you can incorporate the concept of energy into many different parts of your syllabus or science program. Not only does this flexibility make it easier for you to tie together otherwise separate topics, it also helps you stay on track when students bring in their own questions that can be answered through an exploration of energy. In dealing with questions, pick the approach that best fits your syllabus or science program.

Probably the most studied of all children's misconceptions are those they harbor about force and motion. Most children and many adults make an erroneous connection between the two. If an object is moving, then there must be a force making it move. This alternative view has been observed through a variety of different research techniques. It appears to be very widespread and also highly resistant to change. At least if you are aware of the problem you can take steps to correct it. The idea seems to be the result of life long experience with frictional effects. Most people have very limited experience with low friction events. An approach to change this misconception, which has been tested and found to have some success, is to explicitly help students bridge from familiar situations to more abstract, frictionless motion events. If any of the children have played air hockey, you can use that as a way to begin. Perhaps thinking about a ball rolling across a very smooth floor can be a discussion's starting point or even a good demonstration. Sometimes a very simple demonstration can be used to help children examine and refine or correct their naive ideas. Refer back to the vignette in chapter 2. The simple act of throwing a ball up into the air and letting it come back down can be used as part of a powerful lesson in examining one's thoughts and clearing up misconceptions.

Work, energy, force, and motion! Let's look at the following favorite Science Activity to Try that encompasses all of these concepts and more as some sixth graders try to solve some problems.

ENERGY AND WORK

Title: Energy and Work

Skills: Observing, inferring, predicting, hypothesizing, creating models, measuring

Content: Matter, energy, work, change, potential and kinetic energy

Materials: Cartoons—Figures A through D

Procedure: Ask the students to observe Figure A. Lucy is standing at the top of a very high cliff. Stuck at the edge of this cliff is a huge boulder.

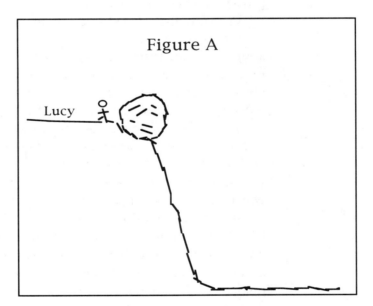

Figure A

Lucy

Ask the questions: Does the boulder have any energy stuck way up there on that cliff? (yes) It's not moving. What kind of energy can it have? (potential) In order for that boulder to do any work, it must have kinetic energy. How can Lucy convert the potential energy the rock has into kinetic energy? (move the boulder) As soon as the boulder has moved the initial tiny distance, what conversion has begun? (some of the potential energy has been converted to kinetic)

As the boulder accelerates down the cliff, what is happening to the amounts of potential and kinetic energy? (as the potential energy decreases, the kinetic energy increases—at the same rate) Show Figure B.

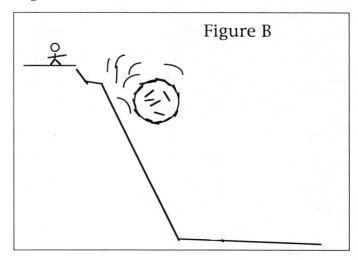

Figure B

In Figure C, the boulder is no longer moving. Ask: Can you describe what has happened to the kinetic energy? (the boulder did all the work it could and the energy was converted back to potential) Since we agree that the boulder now has more potential energy than kinetic, let's look at "the rest of the story."

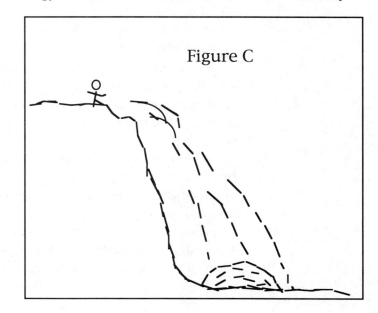

Figure C

Consider the two possible scenarios shown in Figure D.

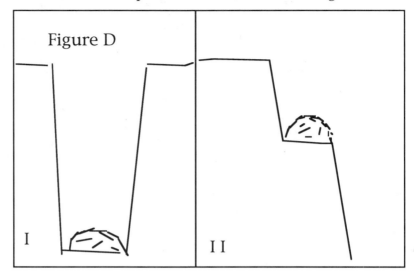

In Figure D- I, the boulder has come to rest in the narrow gorge. In Figure D- II, the boulder has come to rest on the edge of another high cliff. Have the students draw this picture in their notebooks and, in their small groups, have them do some brainstorming and consider the answer to the following question. The boulder in Figure D- I is the same as the one in Figure D- II. The only difference is the position. Is the amount of potential energy in the boulder greater in Figure D- I, greater in Figure D- II, or the same in both?

Ask the children to include a written statement in their notes describing their thinking as they came to a consensus. (The discussion that follows may have groups with different ideas as to the solution to the problem. Conversely, everyone may feel the same way.)

Now, turn imagination into a hands-on science experience. To the class (after each group has proposed its solution): I like your thinking here. Is there some way to demonstrate your choice? Is there a way to find out the actual solution? More discussion.

When real scientists have a problem such as this one, when it is difficult or impossible to actually go to a site where the problem really exists, they try to recreate the problem in their laboratory. This is called replicating or creating a replica. A replica is a model of something built to simulate the real thing. Ask the questions: Is there a way to replicate the scenarios shown in Figure D right here in the classroom so that we can solve our problem? More discussion.

Let's think about the problem and put it in common language. What is energy? (the ability to do work/move matter) In order for one object to have more energy than another, what must it be able to do more of than the other? (work/change or move matter) If we want to find out if an object in one position has more or less energy than an object in another, what must we make the objects do? (work/change or move matter) Spend a few minutes brainstorming with your group and try to find a way we can replicate the problem in the classroom. When you come to a consensus, write your idea down and show it to me.

After more discussion and ideas are shared, guide the thinking to a problem similar to that in Figure D in your notes. If we were going to use the bookshelves as the location of the boulder, is the top shelf similar to Figure D- I or D- II? (D- II) What about the bottom shelf? (D- I) If we use this object (ball) to replicate the boulder, what must happen in order to replicate the problem?

Let's replicate the language of the problem to fit the classroom situation. Does the ball have a different amount of potential energy on the top shelf than it does on the bottom? Or, is there no difference? Go back to where you wrote your opinions about the scenario in Figure D and rewrite it to fit the bookshelf problem. In your group, follow your problem-solving plan to find a solution.

The groups should be guided to test the ball's energy from both heights by giving the ball some work to do. The work can be any type as long as the result can be measured or described in such a way that the solution is evident. (crush paper cups, splash water, move sand, etc.; if the ball crushes more cups, splashes more water from the higher position, moves more sand, it has done more work and, therefore, must have had more energy)

After the observed results are recorded and analyzed, a generalization regarding potential energy and the position of the matter should be forthcoming. Let's refer to the problem presented in Figure D. In situation I, the boulder is stuck. The possibility of it ever moving again is almost zero. In situation II, however, it is easy to see that as soon as some of the dirt holding the boulder in place gets washed away, the boulder has a great chance of falling again. If we think about what we have learned about energy, we can understand that if the boulder in Figure D-I will never be able to do any more work, the potential energy is very low. In Figure D-II the boulder is in a position to fall and do more work. Therefore, it has more potential energy.

Closure: What is potential energy? Kinetic energy? Who can give me examples of these types of energy and how they are a part of your real lives?

The last word that we want to briefly note as causing children difficulties is *machine*. When pressed for a definition, children will often try to use examples as a way of explaining what a machine is. They have a poor conception of a generic, energy-transferring machine. They almost exclusively discuss complex machines like cars, robots, or some other technically advanced device. They don't even consider simple (in the scientific sense) machines like pliers, wheelbarrows, or car jacks. The best bet here is to bring in some small hand tools or similar pieces of equipment for the children to measure and experiment with. Once they can recognize the different types of simple machines, they should be able to take a complex machine and break it down into its component simple machines—just don't bring in a car for them to take apart!

Let's take a quick look at some simple machines!

Levers

You almost certainly want to begin a study of simple machines with an examination of levers. You might ask the children to find all the different ways that a load, a force, and a pivot point could be combined on a long piece of wood. Have them look at which arrangements make it easier and which make it harder to lift the load. If they are thorough (and you can count on it if all class members do the investigation) someone is bound to come up with an example of each of the three classes of levers. (A first-class lever is one where the fulcrum is located anywhere between the force and the resistance; a second-class lever is one where the resistance is between the force and the fulcrum; and a third-class lever is one where the force is between the resistance and the fulcrum.) It is helpful at this stage to have real-world examples of how those levers are used. They will quickly relate to the see-saw in the playground (first class), but also show them nutcrackers (second class), tweezers (third class), scissors (first class), bottle opener (second class), and broom (third class). Ask them how the use of each device affects their design.

This is probably where you want to start talking about energy conservation. Children using a scissors-style car jack to lift a big pile of books will be impressed with the force the jack can apply. Make sure they lift the books a large distance so they begin to see that it still takes energy to do the work. Tell them that they "can't get something for nothing." If they want to get a large force out of a machine like the jack, then they must be willing to apply their small input forces over a very large distance. What they gain in force they lose in distance. If your students are old enough to multiply, they can take a few measurements and verify that the product of the input force and distance is about the same as the resulting force and distance output.

$$F_1 \times d_1 = F_2 \times d_2$$

If they are examining a see-saw, they can discover that the grand total of all weights times distance to pivot points on one side must match the same total on the other side. In other words, the work put out equals the work put in. The "Visual Almanac" videodisc has a very nice set of photographs and interactive tasks to help children make this discovery.

Inclined Planes

Ramps or inclined planes are pretty easy for children to understand. They can slide books on top of other books using short, steep ramps and long, gradual ramps. This will quickly point out the force/distance tradeoff. With inclined planes, less force is used sliding the books along a long, gradual ramp, but it has to be exerted for a longer distance. Moving the books is made easier because at any one moment more of the weight is being supported by the plank and less by the individual's muscles. If any of them have heard that you are more likely to get cut with a dull knife than with a sharp one, ask them why this might be. Draw a cross section of a dull and sharp knife blade and talk about how you have less mechanical advantage with the dull blade and would have to apply more force to cut something, making it more likely to slip and thus be more dangerous.

Inclined planes make work easier by making jobs more gradual. They are simple machines that give us a gain in force. Many examples of inclined planes are found in our everyday world. They include access ramps for the handicapped, the sloping floor of the school auditorium, long stairways, and escalators.

Wheel and Axle

Have you ever noticed the huge steering wheel in the school bus? You can be sure your students have. Ask them to explain why it is different than the one found in their family car. They can make a list of all the wheel and axle machines they can find for a week (pencil sharpener, doorknob, fishing reel, electric can opener, pepper grinder). Bring in a set of well-designed screwdrivers. The students should notice that as the blade (the axle) gets wider, so does the handle diameter (the wheel). If they make measurements of the two dimensions (length and width (diameter)) they will probably be surprised to find that the ratio is fairly consistent. If you can find one, bring in a poorly designed screwdriver with a moderately sized blade but a thin handle. Have children use it and a good screwdriver to drive a screw into a piece of wood. They'll quickly discover the importance of mechanical advantage!

Simple wheel and axle machines are everywhere. When one larger wheel is connected to and turns a smaller wheel or shaft (the axle) you have a machine that gains in force. In other words, a smaller force (or effort) at the wheel will move a larger weight at the axle. With our doorknob example, if you unscrew the knob and try to turn the axle with your hand and open the door, it's difficult to do! Put the knob back on the axle. Now, with just a little effort (force) applied to the knob (wheel), a larger force will be transmitted to the axle and you can open the door with relative ease. Try to think of and explain another common wheel and axle example.

Pulley Secrets

Children love being in on a secret. Start by letting them play with a few small pulley systems to get an intuitive feeling for the long pull needed to lift a heavy weight a short distance. They'll see this as another example of what they learned from experimenting with levers. Then point out that the number of strings supporting the moving pulleys (attached to the load) is also the *force multiplying factor*. If there are five strings to the bottom pulley, they can lift a five-pound book with only a one-pound pull, but to lift it an inch they must pull out five inches of string. Give them a whole series of different pulley arrangements (or drawings of them) and see how quickly they can figure out the mechanical advantage by using the secret of counting strings. It seems silly, but children love it. Watch them stump their friends with pulley-related questions! As with the other simple machines and science in general, hands-on experience can't be beat!

MAGNETISM

Understanding Magnets and Magnetic Fields

For once, children don't seem to have too many misconceptions about a science topic! Your students probably have played with magnets, but they are such unusual (yet simple) things that children usually haven't developed many ideas about them. The most common misconception about magnets is that children believe that *All* metals are attracted by them. Most people don't know how magnets are different from nonmagnetic pieces of metal, so you may want to discuss the matter. (Magnets attract iron and certain other metals because the individual atoms in the metals act like tiny magnets themselves. These tiny magnets are each attached to the magnet. The atoms in nonmagnetic metals (copper, brass, aluminum) have no net magnetic field and are not attracted to the magnet.)

Try the following science activity with your fourth graders to find out more about magnetism, and more specifically, what materials are attracted by magnets and what materials will allow the mysterious force of magnetism to pass through. Remember, a naive conception that children believe is that all metals are attracted by magnets. In this activity, they will discover for themselves that this is not the case. In fact, only iron, nickel, and cobalt (and alloys of these materials) are attracted by a magnet. For an interesting discrepant event in this activity, hide a portion of a straight pin in the yellow sponge and see the look of surprise on students' faces when the yellow sponge is "attracted" by the magnet!

SCIENCE ACTIVITY TO TRY

MYSTERIOUS MAGNETISM

Title: Mysterious Magnetism

Skills: Observing, classifying, predicting, measuring, inferring, hypothesizing, recording data, recognizing variables

Content: Magnetic/nonmagnetic materials, magnetic fields, poles, repulsion, attraction

Materials: Small bar magnets, paper clips, assorted materials such as copper, cloth, acetate (from overhead masters), waxed paper, emery cloth, aluminum foil, paper, brass, blue and yellow sponges, record sheets

Procedure: Organize assorted materials for pick-up cafeteria style. Request students to predict (on their record sheets) if (1) the material is magnetic (i.e., is attracted by the magnet), and (2) magnetism will pass through the material. Demonstrate operational definitions for each of these procedures.

Record class predictions on the board, by numbers of yes and no predictions. Pass out the materials and review each test item. Pass out the magnets and paper clips and encourage investigation. Encourage investigation of objects in addition to those provided. Collect all materials and clean up.

Closure: Record findings on the board and discuss what conclusions can be made about items that are attracted by magnets and magnetism passing through items. What hypothesis can be made about magnetism?

Magnetism Record Sheet

For each of the objects below, place a check (✓) in the appropriate column predicting whether the item is attracted by the magnet and whether magnetism will pass through it. Then, use a magnet to test your predictions and record your results.

	MAGNETIC?		DOES MAGNETISM PASS THROUGH?	
ITEM	YES	NO	YES	NO
Emery Cloth				
Acetate				
Waxed Paper				
Copper Foil				
Felt				
Aluminum Foil				
Paper				
Brass Foil				
Blue Sponge				
Yellow Sponge				

1. What conclusions can you make about objects that are attracted by magnets?

2. What conclusions can you make about magnetism passing through objects?

3. What hypothesis can you make about magnetism?

Everyone's favorite way to study magnetic fields is to play with iron filings. This can be a messy affair, so be prepared. You might want to put your magnets into Ziploc plastic bags so that they don't get covered with filings. You can even work with an overhead projector if you like but don't keep all the fun to yourself. Let the children work with and draw the magnetic fields from single magnets and pairs of magnets with like or opposite poles placed near each other. If you can get small compasses, they can be used to map out the field near a bar or horseshoe magnet. Tape a magnet to the inside of a shoebox lid. By using compasses or filings, children can deduce the location of the hidden magnet.

After your students have enough experience with magnets that they firmly believe that opposite poles attract and like poles repel, ask them the following question: "Why does the north end of a compass point to the north pole of the earth? Shouldn't it be repelled?" That not only will get them thinking, it will probably also stump their parents when the children bring it up at supper. Many people have never thought of this little question. But once it's been pointed out to them, they get quite confused because they thought they understood magnets pretty well. Of course, the truth is that the earth has it's south magnetic pole in Hudson Bay, near the geographic north pole. The north magnetic pole is in Antarctica. The north end of compasses is called "north" because that is the (geographic) north-seeking end. But it is attracted to magnetic south poles.

To help students understand how magnets work, have them combine a bunch of small, weak magnets into a larger and stronger magnet. This is similar to the way atoms line up in a metal as it is magnetized. Have them make a new magnet by stroking a large nail with a magnet. Stroking the metal with a magnet makes the individual iron atoms line up, just like a compass follows a magnet. The minuscule magnetism of each atom adds to that of its neighbors, producing a sizable magnetic field. Once they test their magnetized nail, have them hit it with a hammer a few times. They'll discover that it isn't a magnet anymore (or at least it is much weaker than it was). That is because they have "rattled" the iron atoms so much that the atoms no longer line up like they did. It would be like taking the small magnets apart so they no longer formed the stronger combination magnet. If you've already covered heat and described it as vibrations of atoms, students can experience that by seeing that their nail loses its magnetism when it is heated, causing its atoms to vibrate out of alignment.

Electromagnets

Let's look at how one teacher has his students investigate the topic of electromagnetism. Think about how you would cover the same material.

Ms. Robinson: OK, class, let's focus our attention up here. Who remembers what our science assignment was for last night?

Linda: We had to be magnetism detectives!

Ms. Robinson: Right! Why don't we make a list of places at home where you found magnets.

Jim: I've got an easy one . . . on the refrigerator!

Ms. Robinson: OK. I assume you mean your family uses magnets to hold messages up on the door of the refrigerator. Let's write that down. What about the refrigerator itself? Remember we said that many things that plug into an electrical outlet use magnetism. [Pauses 15 to 20 seconds.] Sally?

Sally: Is there some kind of motor inside? Ours hums sometimes if I forget to close the door. Is that a motor making that noise?

Ms. Robinson: Yes, it is. There is an electric motor that runs something called a compressor that helps cool the food inside. Electric motors usually have electromagnets in them. Good. Anyone else?

Marvin: I found a vacuum cleaner and a clock radio. I know there's a motor in the vacuum cleaner. Is there one in the clock radio?

Ms. Robinson: You're right about the vacuum. Does the clock radio have a regular clock face or does it have one of those red digital numbers?

Marvin: It's got the red numbers.

Ms. Robinson: Well, there's no motor then. Regular clocks have motors that turn the hands around the dial. I bet there is still a magnet in there somewhere, though. Does anyone know where? [long pause] It's in the radio speaker! There is an electromagnet that uses the electricity coming out of the radio circuit to wiggle a round piece of paper. That wiggling paper makes the air move . . . and you've got sound. Has anybody ever seen the inside of a speaker?

Jill: I saw my brother's stereo speakers when he was putting them in his car. They had great big magnets in them. He wouldn't let me touch them, though!

Ms. Robinson: He was probably afraid that the paper part of the speaker would get damaged. If it gets a hole poked in it, the speaker is ruined.

Jill: Hey, aren't there magnets in his cassette player? He told me to keep his tapes away from the speakers 'cuz he said they were magnetically recorded. But cassette tapes are plastic or something, aren't they?

Ms. Robinson: Yes, they are. But tiny metal particles are attached to the plastic. Electromagnets inside the player can detect how they are magnetized and turn that into music.

Jill: But his stereo has a button that says *chrome tape*. Are those tapes different?

Ms. Robinson: A little bit. When they are being recorded, the circuit controlling the electromagnet has to send a special signal—called a bias signal—to the tape.

Marvin: What's it do?

Ms. Robinson: Remember when we sprinkled iron filings onto a paper that was covering a magnet? Do you remember how tapping the paper helped the filings line up with the magnetic field? That's kind of like how the bias recording signal works. It helps the little particles line up the way the music says they should.

Marvin: Awesome!

Ms. Robinson: Right! Now, are there any other magnets in a cassette player?

Why did the teacher spend so much time talking about a cassette player? (And where did she learn all that stuff, anyway?!) Do you think that this detracted from the lesson? What do you need to think about as you decide how much detail to include in a lesson? Is a teacher-centered discussion the way to go in a problems approach science program?

Motors and Generators

A natural way to move a class along from a discussion of magnetism to the topic of electricity is by having the students explore motors and generators. If you can purchase one of the kits or you can find a set of plans, your class can actually build little motors. (Talk to a technology teacher at a nearby junior high school). If you have a

Teflon stirring bar (like the kind described in the vignette in Chapter 5), you can have your students spin it very rapidly by waving a strong horseshoe magnet near it. This experience can be extended by mentioning that electromagnets take the place of the permanent magnets in most real motors. If you have an old kitchen mixer or some other motorized device, take it apart to show the children the armature (a metal piece above the poles of the electric magnet) and field coils (insulated wire that is wrapped around the piece of soft iron called the *core*), but don't plug it in while it is apart!

Many motors made from kits can also work as simple generators, although they may not produce very much energy. If desired, you can either purchase or make a simple galvanometer to measure these small currents. If you bought the motor kits, the same supply house should sell galvanometers. If you want your students to build one, take a look at the *Science Scope* article (Beichner, 1990) cited at the end of this chapter. Building such a device is not a bad science investigation on its own as a fifth- or sixth-grade activity.

ELECTRICITY

Shocking Misconceptions!

Elementary school children have been using electricity for a long time and they have some pretty stable ideas about how it works. The convenience of electrical outlets on every wall has led to quite a few mistaken impressions of where electricity comes from. A lot of children think it somehow appears in the socket or comes out from inside the wall. Rather than needing a circuit, electricity somehow flows through the cord into the electrical device, where it is used up. (This would be analogous to refilling an automobile with gasoline.) The fact that electricity seems to be some sort of fluid means that children think that it needs wires to carry it. Another misconception that you need to be watching for stems from the fact that electricity is very common. Because children are literally surrounded by electricity, they sometimes tend to think that it is not very dangerous. Make sure they are taught to be cautious around electricity and that they are aware of safety issues like proper plugging and unplugging of cords, limiting the number of plugs in one socket, keeping electrical appliances away from water, and so on.

Exploring Static Electricity

Some of your children may have already played with tiny bits of paper and a comb. At some time they certainly have taken a balloon, rubbed it in their hair, and stuck the balloon to the wall. Most will have "discovered" static electricity after shuffling across a rug and touching a doorknob. These common experiences can be used as a springboard to a more detailed examination of static electricity. Closer observations of paper being attracted to a comb reveal that after a few moments it jumps away from the comb, not just falling off, but actually being repelled. Your students will want to know why this happens. (If you don't already know the answer, it's time to work on building up your data base of teaching ideas again; static electricity is caused by the gain or loss of electrons. Some substances tend to gain electrons easily; other substances tend to lose them easily. When two different substances are brought close together (by rubbing) electrons can move from one to the other. When one object gains electrons, it has a surplus of electrons and has a negative charge. When one object loses electrons, it has a shortage of electrons and has a positive charge. Most anything will generate some sort of charge when rubbed. Now, what about our comb and paper activity? By rubbing the comb, it becomes charged and attracts the uncharged paper bits. After a while, the paper bits jump off again. Why? When those bits of paper touch the comb, they gradually take on the same charge as the comb. At that point, they have like charges. Since like charges repel, the paper bits jump away. Use this teacher information wisely; promote discussion of ideas that may lead to further activities and more observation so that the children attain this concept for themselves. Don't be a Ms. Robinson all the time!)

When working with balloons, have your students tape the ends of a long, thin string or thread to a pair of balloons. After charging both balloons by rubbing them in their hair, they should lift the two balloons by holding onto the center of the thread. The children will be able to see that the two balloons repel each other. If you can get some fur and plastic or silk and glass, you can apply opposite charges to balloons to show their attraction. (Rub the plastic with the fur and bring the plastic close to one balloon; charge the other balloon by rubbing the glass with silk and bringing the glass close to the balloon. Now bring the two balloons close together.) There are all kinds of fascinating static electricity activities. Allow your students some free investigating to devise others!

Electrical Currents

Children are much less likely to have extended experience with electrical currents. Of course they have played with battery- operated toys and have used devices that operate on electrical current, but your students have been somewhat removed from the current itself, mostly for safety reasons. When exploring electric current in the classroom, use low-power flashlight batteries (D-cell batteries work well) as a source of current. The classic experiment is to give children a battery, a bulb, and a single piece of wire. (Look back to the Science Activity to Try in Chapter 3.) The goal is to light the bulb. This can be extended to series and parallel connections of bulbs, helping to break down the idea that current is "used up" in electrical devices.

An inexpensive demonstration of an electrical generator can be found in your local department store in the toy department. A bicycle light system with a generator that rubs against the tire can be purchased for just a few dollars. A quick rubbing of the generator along the edge of a rug or similar large, nonslippery surface should be sufficient to briefly light the bulb. You can usually dismantle the generator to see what is inside. (Many children expect to find a battery.) If you would rather talk about producing electricity by converting chemical energy rather than mechanical, you can make a battery from a lemon and copper and zinc strips of metal. If you have trouble obtaining those materials, make a somewhat less powerful battery by dangling (from separate wires) a copper penny and a steel washer into a glass of salt water. Attach the other ends of the wires to a galvanometer and you should be able to detect a current. If you want to take this idea to the extreme, you can even get a potato clock from some novelty shops. By pushing two short nails made of dissimilar metals into a potato, you can actually get enough electrical current to run a small, efficient clock motor. You can also buy little solar cells and use them to produce electricity. In bright light a single cell should easily be able to drive a tiny electric motor. All of these sources of electricity should be used to emphasize that electrical energy is being produced from the conversion of some other form of energy. It doesn't just appear. The force that drives the current has to come from somewhere.

LOOKING BACK

Machines, magnetism, and electricity are among the most practically oriented of all the science topics. You should have no trouble bringing in examples of simple machines or helping students think up places where electricity and magnetism make their lives easier. Make as many connections to their everyday lives as possible. Many students naturally gravitate toward these engineering-oriented subjects. Encourage their interest.

SELF-TEST

- What are some of the misconceptions children have about machines, magnetism, and electricity?

- What is potential energy? Kinetic energy? Can you give examples of each?

- Can you list some of the basic, simple machines and examples of their use in real-life?

- Discuss some of the misconceptions children have with the concept of electricity.

- How are magnets different from nonmagnetic pieces of metal?

SCOPE AND SEQUENCE

Possibilities for coverage are listed here; as usual, modify the list as necessary.

Kindergarten   Movement and machines

First grade   Motion and work, magnets

Second grade   Simple machines, electricity, electromagnets

Third grade   Energy and machines, types of energy, compasses

Fourth grade   Work and energy, static electricity, magnetism

Fifth grade   Types of simple machines, electrical circuits, batteries, Cause of magnetism

Sixth grade   Energy conservation, electrical energy, electrical equipment

REFERENCES FROM RESEARCH

Barrow, L. (1987, July). *Magnet concepts and elementary students' misconceptions.* Proceedings of the Second International Seminar on Misconceptions and Educational Strategies in Science and Mathematics, Ithaca, N.Y.: Cornell University, pp.17–22.

Clement, J. (1982). Students' preconceptions in introductory physics. *American Journal of Physics*, 50(1), 66–71.

Johsua, S. and Dupin, J. J. (1987). Taking into account student conceptions in instructional strategy: an example in physics. *Cognition and Instruction*, 4(2), 117–135.

Steinberg, M. (1983, June). *Reinventing electricity.* Proceedings of the International Seminar on Misconceptions and Educational Strategies in Science and Mathematics, Ithaca, N.Y.: Cornell University, pp. 388–401.

PRACTICAL RESOURCES

Beichner, R. J. (1990). Paper cup magnetism. *Science Scope*, 52, 18–19.

Lunetta, V. and Novick, S. (1982). *Inquiring and problem-solving in the physical sciences: a sourcebook.* Dubuque, Iowa: Kendall/Hunt.

The Visual Almanac videodisc is available from Optical Data Corporation, 30 Technology Drive, Warren, NJ 07059.

Magnets (and lots of other neat stuff) are available from Edmund Scientific, 101 E. Gloucester Pike, Barrington, NJ 08007-1380, (609) 573–6253.

Radio Shack is an excellent source for wire, small bulbs, batteries, and most other components for simple circuits.

9   Science in the Community and Everyday Life

LOOKING AHEAD

Why do you want your students to learn science? Besides the obvious answer that science is in the syllabus or school program, there are other very important reasons to learn about science topics. From its very beginning, our country has depended on an informed citizenry to make important decisions like choosing (electing) government officials. Today's need for a scientifically literate electorate is greater than it has ever been. Many difficult questions have been raised because of our advancing technology. As we struggle to find the best ways to reduce our adverse impact on the environment and also address the ethical issues brought about by state-of-the-art medicine, it becomes apparent that the road to answers runs through the classroom. It is only by fostering an understanding of both scientific knowledge and the methodology of science that we can hope to find solutions to many of the problems facing the world today and in the future.

Finally, before we close, focus on the following questions that make you refocus your thoughts on science teaching and apply your teaching endeavors to problems in the real world.

CAN YOU?

- State three important reasons for teaching science to children?

- Help children apply scientific reasoning to their everyday lives?

- Suggest how a knowledge of science can affect your students' present and future role in the community?

UNDERSTANDING CURRENT EVENTS

For a few moments, place this book aside and take a look at the first few pages of today's newspaper. What do you see? Many of the issues and events described there have a scientific origin. To even begin to understand what they are about requires a significant background in science. Unfortunately, many Americans are woefully ignorant of even basic scientific facts. This is a double indictment of our schools. First, many students are able to graduate with minimal exposure to science. Second, and possibly even more critical, most students leave school with no interest in scientific topics. If the first problem were resolved, we would have a population better able to deal with the issues of the day, basing their opinions and actions on direct knowledge (or knowing how to search for answers). If the second shortcoming were addressed, even if a particular current event involved a science area where any given person had little prior understanding, the person would probably be interested enough to follow the story and search out ways to learn more about its content.

Let's examine a few of the most important science-related issues facing our nation and world and take a look at how you might teach about them in your classroom.

ENERGY CONCERNS

The Use of Fossil Fuels

A good way to start children talking about the use of fossil fuels is to discuss the term *fossil fuels*. Without explanation, this can be a very confusing phrase. It might even be possible to bring in a lump of coal with a small fossil in it. If you can find such a piece, by all means bring it in. It will act as a concrete reminder of what fossil fuels are and where they came from. Passing it around the room will probably result in enough smudged fingers that students won't have any difficulty understanding why improper coal use can cause pollution. When discussing other fossil fuels, make sure students realize that natural gas is not gasoline. They can get the two terms mixed up because people tend to call gasoline "gas" even though it is a liquid.

One of the most important points to impress upon your students is the limited supply of fossil fuels that are available for use. They aren't going to understand Hubbert demand curves, but they really don't need to. To get across the idea of how our oil and natural gas resources are being used, take a sponge and get it very wet. Hold it up (over a wash basin) and students will see water dripping from it. This is equivalent to the famous oil "gushers" that only need to be tapped and oil comes out because of subterranean pressures. There are similar wells and even naturally occurring springs of natural gas. Ask students how long the water will continue to drip out. By the time you ask the question, it may have stopped! Now pose the problem of getting more water out. You won't have to wait long before someone tells you to squeeze the sponge. Do so, but with a light touch. Lots of water should run into the basin. Have your students relate this to pumping oil and natural gas out of the ground. Once this easy supply is out of the sponge, students are bound to tell you to squeeze harder. When you do this, with obvious effort, make the connection to working harder to extract oil and gas resources. Ask the students how this might affect the price of these resources. This is roughly equivalent to where we are now in the recovery of these resources. After this moderate squeezing, only strenuous wringing will bring any more water out of the sponge. As your students should note, this will be very expensive when done in the real world. When you have gotten every last drop of water out that you can, pass the sponge around the room. Students will discover that it still contains water, they just aren't able to get it all out. This is analogous to the situation where oil and natural gas will be so expensive to recover that we will have to find alternatives. Even though some of the resources are still in the ground, we will have neither the technology nor the money to retrieve them.

After students have a good understanding of our limited supply of oil and natural gas, ask them to find out how people are trying to reduce our dependence on these natural resources. If you can find some photographs of cars from the 1960s and 1970s, bring them in and have students compare their design to that of today's cars. Ask if any of their parents turn down the thermostat at night or have added insulation to the attic. Be sure to mention how important it is to turn out the lights when leaving a room! This seems to be a continual problem with youngsters. One way to help them remember the rule is to explain why it is there in the first place. The largest percentage of energy use is in the home (including that for family transportation).

At some point, you should also talk about the pollution problems associated with the burning of hydrocarbon fuels. Compare the cleanliness of oil burning to that of coal and natural gas. Have your students find out which fuel(s) are used to generate the electricity for their homes. Relate the discussion back to the demonstration with the sponge. We are in the "harder squeeze" stage with oil and natural gas. We are still in the "easy squeeze" phase with coal, but, unfortunately, it can be a dirty fuel. Natural gas is the cleanest burning of all the fossil fuels, but also the least abundant.

You might want to do a Home Energy Audit with your students. First, have them rank the following items according to how much energy they (their family) use during the year:

Hot water heater

Household lights

Air conditioning

Refrigerator-freezer

Television

Clothes dryer

Clothes washer

Clocks

Range

Toaster

Do this in groups, so that debate occurs. Next, give the students some homework; have them research their own home energy use over the past year. Many utilities provide energy summaries right on their billing statements. Have students work with their parents on the ranking of the ten household energy users. Discuss the results of their Home Energy Audits. (Generally, heating and cooling the home are the major energy users; heating water, the refrigerator-freezer, household lights, range, clothes dryer, television, clothes washer, toaster, and clocks should fill out the list; the biggest energy users are those things that are on most of the time.)

Trying Renewable Energy Sources
There will probably be a resurgence of interest in renewable energy sources as our fossil fuels become more expensive. Depending on your location, there might already be substantial use of these alternative sources of energy (solar, wind, geothermal, etc.). If there are, perhaps you can arrange a field trip or at least bring in some photographs or newspaper articles about the facility.

Children in elementary school can easily construct a solar collector from an insulated box with a plastic cover. If it is lined with black paper and a thermometer is placed inside, appreciable temperature increases will be seen even on a cool day, as long as it is sunny. If you want to demonstrate electrical conversion, pick up a few solar cells at a local electronic parts store such as Radio Shack. These can be used to operate a small electric motor, as was mentioned in Chapter 8. Currently, this type of energy production is not very efficient and so can be quite expensive on a large scale.

If the little motor you used for the solar electricity experiment spins freely enough, you might be able to turn it into a wind-driven electrical generator by the addition of a large cardboard propeller. There are also some good short films that demonstrate the use of wind energy to generate electricity. An interesting use of wind-generated electricity is to break water down into hydrogen and oxygen. The hydrogen can be used as a fuel, much as natural gas or gasoline are used now. The by-product of its combustion is water vapor. This eventually falls back down as rain and can be used as a source of hydrogen again. The energy comes from the wind, but it is stored in the hydrogen. It is counted as a renewable energy source because the hydrogen is not used up and is available (in water) as more fuel.

If you live in an agricultural region, you might be able to find information about biomass energy conversion. These techniques use agricultural products to produce fuel like gasohol or methane gas. A field trip to a farm where this is being done could not only show children how biomass energy is being used but also expose them to all the life science found on a farm.

Investigating Nuclear Energy

Children, if they have any opinions of nuclear energy, tend to be afraid of it. They don't really grasp the difference between the controlled release of energy from a reactor and the uncontrolled explosion of a nuclear weapon. You might want to relate the reactor to an automobile engine. Gasoline is dangerous if not handled properly, but when used in a car engine, the energy contained in the fuel is released slowly and with a great deal of operator control. The same is true of nuclear energy. The fuel is dangerous and can be used to create powerful weapons, but under controlled conditions, the energy released from nuclear fission can be used to generate electricity. Of course, the biggest problem for the nuclear industry is the long-term storage of spent fuel, which is radioactive material. This has not been satisfactorily solved yet. Some people think that until this difficulty is resolved (assuming it can be), nuclear power production should be curtailed. Regardless of your own position on this issue (or any other, for that matter), it is your duty as a teacher to fully inform your students of the arguments on all sides of the controversy. If it really were completely one sided, there wouldn't be much to argue about. You have a tremendous power to influence the thoughts of young people. Recognize that capability and don't abuse it!

DEALING WITH POLLUTION

Today's children seem to be aware of the impact of humans on the environment. Most are quite motivated and willing to learn what they can do to "help the earth." But be gentle when outlining the possible effects of habitat destruction and overpopulation. Yes, children need to learn about rainforest depletion and endangered species, but don't give them nightmares. Focus more on what can be done now instead of what has happened in the past. Also, let them know that there is natural pollution—such as radon gas and volcanic eruptions. People have been the "bad guys" in the past, but we still have a chance to mend our ways!

Threats to Our Air and Water Supplies

A nice way to introduce children to the need to care for our surroundings is by keeping a classroom hamster (or gerbil). Children quickly discover that the little animal works hard to keep its food and water separate from its own waste. You can ask your students about this and why it is so important. Talk about what people can do to keep residential and industrial waste away from our food supplies. Water is one of our most precious resources. It is practically inexhaustible, but water conservation and solutions to water pollution are of great importance. Don't forget to mention air pollution and what is being done about it. Air, like water, is inexhaustible, but good, clean air is becoming scarcer. Industrial air pollution from acid rain to photochemical smog to chlorofluorocarbons (CFCs) have an adverse impact on the earth's atmosphere and on the survival of humans. Discuss places where your students have seen pollution and what they might be able to do about it. These problems are very complex, but a scientifically literate populace is a good beginning to solutions.

The Issue of Global Warming

Global warming is a not a difficult concept for children. Almost all have experienced an overheated car that was left in a sunny parking lot without rolling down a window. They can make their own miniature greenhouses by using two Styrofoam cups, each holding the same amount of water and a thermometer. They should put one in a tightly closed plastic bag. Then they place both cups on a sunny windowsill. It won't take long for the sun to raise the temperature inside the sealed system. This is analogous to carbon dioxide letting sunlight in to the earth's surface, but not letting as much heat escape.

The problem of global warming due to the greenhouse effect (there is much carbon dioxide in the earth's atmosphere due to pollution; this carbon dioxide traps solar radiation and, consequently, heats up the atmosphere) is a serious, very complex environmental problem. This is a problem that affects students' lives. They can do something about it. From simply conserving energy to making their voices heard on issues related to global warming, they can act.

What about Ozone Depletion

Ozone depletion is not as easy to explain to children as global warming. They can't see or feel the effect of a change in the earth's protective ozone layer. If the children live in a metropolitan area, they may have heard that ozone is a pollutant near ground level. Yet it is a necessary component of the upper atmosphere. This can be very confusing. Perhaps they'll understand that the ozone—a special form of oxygen (O_3)—acts like the sunscreen lotion they should be using when they go to the beach. It keeps harmful rays from the sun from reaching the earth. This protective layer of the upper atmosphere is disappearing because of the current use of certain chemical products, especially CFC propellants (the stuff used in spray cans, refrigerants for cars and refrigerators, and the material used to make Styrofoam egg cartons and fast-food packaging). These pollutants are moving up into the protective ozone layer and causing it to break down. You might want to discuss some of the recent news articles on this important topic.

Promoting Recycling

Children generally respond very well to instruction on recycling and caring for the environment. When you think about it, these concepts are not much different (to the children, at least) than putting their toys away and cleaning their rooms. Children seem more than willing to jump on the bandwagon and take care of the planet. In fact, what often happens is that a child will end up changing their family's behavior by pointing out to parents the need for recycling and reducing waste and pollution. Mom and Dad, with no real way of defending their prior habits, start saving newspapers and putting tin cans and glass bottles into separate containers for recycling! Every little bit eases the load on our overburdened landfills.

A fun way to teach children how materials can be used over and over is to have the class make their own recycled paper. Simply tear up newsprint into very small pieces, let them soak in water for an hour or so, and then use a hand mixer or blender to turn the paper bits into a mush. (If you are using printed newsprint, be aware that the ink will be hard to clean out of the blender!) Mix in a little laundry starch and scoop the pulp up between two pieces of window screen. Squeeze out the water by pressing the screen/pulp/screen "sandwich" between sheets of newspaper or towels. Let it dry overnight and the children should be able to flex the screen away from a sheet of recycled paper. They can write their names or even color a picture on their homemade paper.

Now try the recycling concept with sixth graders and another reusable material: plastics!

SCIENCE ACTIVITY TO TRY

PLASTICS IN OUR WORLD

Title: Plastics in Our World

Skills: Observing, inferring, classifying, collecting, recording and analyzing data, predicting, hypothesizing

Content: Recycling, plastics, physical properties, human technology

Materials: Assorted plastic containers, water, sugar, isopropyl (rubbing) alcohol, dishwashing liquid, scissors and/or metal snips, safety goggles, containers (transparent), plastic bags

Procedure: Hold up a large, plastic item (of your choice from the large assortment available) and ask: How can we tell whether this plastic item can be recycled? Brainstorm and write student answers on the board. Ask how the code number in the triangular symbol on the bottom of the item helps us determine its recyclability. Discussion. Break the students into groups of three or four and give each group a collection of plastic containers. Challenge each group to design a system to match containers lacking recycling codes to their appropriately numbered counterparts using the following testing method: Prepare l inch by l inch plastic chips in advance (from the assorted plastic containers that you collected) and pass out to the groups of children sets of different chips in Ziploc plastic bags. Each bag distributed should contain one chip having a recycling (resin) code on it (usually the bottom of the container). The other chips in each bag should contain unmarked chips representing different samples of each recycling code (keep it simple and don't use codes 4 and 7). Generally, soft-drink bottles are #1; milk jugs are #2; glass cleaner, shampoo, and salad dressing bottles are #3; plastic bags are #4; yogurt cups and rigid bottle caps are #5; prescription bottles are #6; and #7 items made of mixed plastics, such as microwave dishes, are #7. Be sure to include unmarked chips of the same plastic as the coded chip for that bag.

Now, each group can work out procedures for determining which unmarked chips match the coded chip in the bag. Once they've had a stab at doing it themselves, have them share their different procedural plans. They should have derived a classification scheme to separate any chip.

As the students develop their plans for identifying unknown plastics, help them to move toward a procedure similar to the following:

1. Check the bottom of each plastic container in your set for a bull's eye mark or a pinched (raised) line. Record for each container which type of mark is present.

2. Cut a small piece at least l inch by l inch from each container or bottle. Make it into a chip by trimming the corners. Characterize its translucency (e.g., opaque, shiny, dull).

3. Try to bend each piece of plastic with your fingers. Record whether it bends easily or resists bending, remains bent, or returns to its original shape, cracks, and so on.

4. Place each chip in the sugar solution (dissolve 5 level teaspoons (25 gm) of sugar into 2 ½ oz (75 cc) of water for each student team). Record whether the chip floats or sinks.

5. After drying the piece, place it in the solution of water and rubbing alcohol (mix l tablespoon (l5 cc) of rubbing alcohol

with enough water to make 3 oz (100 cc) of liquid, and add a drop of dishwashing liquid for each student team). Record whether the chip floats or sinks.

The following table, adapted from a publication of the Society of the Plastics Industry, Inc., can be compared to your students' results.

			RECYCLING CODE		
Tests	1	2	3	5	6
Bottom mark	Bull's eye	Pinched line	Pinched line	Pinched line	Pinched line
Visual	Clear, waxy	Opaque, waxy	Leather-like, shiny or dull	White, shiny; or hard, waxy	Crystalline or glass-like
Bending	Bends	Stiff, but holds partial curl	Curls and springs back	Flexes back to original position	Bends, but cracks
Buoyancy (sugar water)	Sinks	Floats	Sinks	Floats	Floats
Buoyancy (alcohol water)	Sinks	Floats	Sinks	Floats	Sinks

Adapted from a publication of the Society of the Plastics Industry, Inc.

Did your students implement any new procedures to test the containers? Have them label all unmarked containers with the number they believe appropriate on the basis of their physical tests.

Closure: Discussion questions include the following: What methods, other than chemical tests, might be used to separate from one another different types of plastic? Why is it important in recycling plastics to sort them first by number? Why might some manufacturers resist attempts to require all plastic containers to be labeled by number? Did all of the plastic containers fit into a code category? Why might some plastics not fall clearly into the categories that have been established?

LEARNING TO MAKE WISE DECISIONS

Critically Judging the Claims of Others

After years of exposure to superhuman characters in comic books and on television, it is no wonder that children have difficulty separating fact from fiction. Part of your task as a science teacher should be to show them how to evaluate what others say from a rational perspective. Try to encourage them to examine suspicious claims using the methodology of science: Decide what the question or challenge is, go out and observe, collect and record information, look at the information (analyze it), and decide what to do (come to some conclusion). That's science!

Here's a fun demonstration/experiment to try with your students. Bring in a very large sheet of cardboard to act as a shield. Cut a hole in the middle of it, just big enough for a child to put a hand through. You stand behind the cardboard (so you can't see the children) while different student volunteers place their hands through the hole. Without seeing anything but their hands, you can tell boys from girls. (A female's index finger is longer than her ring finger. On males it's the other way around.) After you have demonstrated your "supernatural" ability, have them see if they can determine how you figured out gender from hand shape. You might need to give them a clue or two, but it will help you start a discussion of sex characteristics in a nonthreatening way. It teaches them to be skeptical when someone claims to have special powers. Of course, the central point here is that you are raising an interesting question that they can answer by careful observations of nature. Astute observations are the key to science and solving problems!

Students Like to Form Their Own Opinions

Children enjoy being given the opportunity to have their own ideas about controversial topics. The adults they see always seem to be expressing their opinions, but youngsters are seldom listened to in discussions about issues of the day. If you stress the importance of justifying personal opinions with a knowledge of the facts on all sides of the argument, you can help children be a part of "adult" discussions. Being able to take up such a role can do a great deal for a child's self-esteem. Certainly youngsters can't argue as forcefully as a seasoned debater, but many adults are pleased to see children who can state their ideas clearly and explain why they feel the way they do.

An important part of learning about issues such as energy sources and the environment is that students begin to consider some of the consequences of their actions. For example, they might persuade their friends not to release helium balloons at a birthday party because animals can eat the deflated balloons and die. We've already talked about how children can influence their families to begin recycling. Don't miss the fact that public opinion can be a powerful influence on corporate America. Groups of children writing letters to local companies about their environmental practices actually can make a difference.

SEEING SCIENCE IN THE WORLD AROUND THEM

The hope hidden between the lines throughout this book is that by carefully structuring what you teach about science and how you teach it, your students can learn to enjoy science and continue to add to their understanding of it throughout their lives. By encouraging their natural interest in their surroundings, further pursuit of scientific knowledge might become a goal for them. Maybe some of them will even decide to take up scientific careers. That would be great, but just as important is developing a generation of Americans who are interested in and understand science as it relates to their lives.

LOOKING BACK

The material discussed in this chapter will probably permeate all of your science lessons. One of the fundamental reasons for teaching science is to help students see how it surrounds them and influences their daily lives. Since scientific concerns are so prevalent, it is important that they learn about them and discover ways to make intelligent decisions. Your influence is extremely powerful. Be sure you teach children how to apply scientific reasoning and knowledge to the problems they will be facing as adults.

SELF-TEST

- What would your Home Energy Audit look like? Rank the list of household energy users listed on p. 170 according to how much energy they consume during the year.

- Describe what global warming is all about.

- What about ozone depletion?

- How can a solid background of science affect your students' present and future role in the community?

PRACTICAL RESOURCES

Endless summer: living with the greenhouse effect. (1988). *Discover,* October.

The greenhouse effect. (1986). *Science Activities,* 23 (1): 23–31.

Hocking, C., et al. (1990). *Global warming & the greenhouse effect,* Great Explorations in Math and Science (GEMS), Lawrence Hall of Science, University of California at Berkeley.

Jones, P. and Wigley, T. (1990). Global warming trends. *Scientific American,* August, 84–91.

New York Science, Technology and Society Education Project. (1992). *Solid waste: is there a solution?* Albany, N.Y.: Research Foundation of the State University of New York.

White, R. (1990). The great climate debate. *Scientific American,* July, 36–43.
For a discussion of the Science, Technology, and Society (STS) versus Content debate, see the September 1991 issue of *NSTA Reports!* National Science Teachers Association, 1742 Connecticut Ave., NW, Washington, DC 20009.

Helping your child learn science is available free by sending your name and address to Department 611X, Consumer Information Center, Pueblo, CO 81009. It contains basic science information, community activities, and a list of recommended books and magazines for children.

LAST, LOOKING AHEAD

Take the thoughts, suggestions, science teaching hints, and science content from this text and assimilate this information into your emerging teaching personality. Much of teaching you can plan for; however, at least part of teaching is spontaneous. Go with the moment. Be prepared. Be ready content- and methods-wise to go with the moment. You'll be taking some teaching risks, but sometimes the rewards for you and your students will be great. Good science teaching!

Index